the Communion of Possibility

Charles E. Winquist

NEW HORIZONS PRESS

753003

Copyright © 1975 by Charles E. Winquist. All Rights Reserved, including all translation rights. No part of this publication may be repro-
duced, stored in a retrieval system, or transmitted, in any form or by
any means, electronic, mechanical, photocopying, recording, or otherwise, except for brief passages in reviews or scholarly essays, without
prior written permission of the publisher.

Printed in the U.S.A.

New Horizons Press
P. O. Box 1758
Chico, CA 95926

Library of Congress Cataloging in Publication Data

Winquist, Charles E   1944-
    The communion of possibility.

    (The religious quest ; v. 2)
    1. Religion and language. 2. Hermeneutics.
3. Church. I. Title. II. Series.
BL65.L2W52   201'.1   75-859
ISBN 0-914914-057
ISBN 0-914914-049 pbk.

for Diane and Heidi

Acknowledgment. Chapter II, "The Sacrament of the Word of God," appeared previously in *Encounter* (Summer 1972), Vol. 33, No. 3, pp.217-229.

THE RELIGIOUS QUEST

Reappraisals of the religious foundations of mankind, both from within religious traditions and from outside of them

Volume One

The Quest for Meaning of Svāmī Vivekānanda
by George M. Williams

Volume Two

The Communion of Possibility
by Charles E. Winquist

CONSULTING EDITORS

Robert Baird
 The University of Iowa
Alan Berger
 Syracuse University
Willard Johnson
 California State Unviersity,
 Long Beach
William Murnion
 Ramapo Colege of
 New Jersey

TABLE OF CONTENTS

FOREWORD

It is a great pleasure, and a privilege, to write a brief foreword to Professor Winquist's new book. This will be an important book, a genuine addition to the discussion of the place and role of religious language and so of theology in modern experience. It is, moreover, unique, at least in the American discussion of religious language, in that it carries its justification of religious language all the way through into a quite distinctive and creative interpretation of the Church as the home for that language, the locus of proclamation and so as the "communion of possibility." Like Bultmann and Moltmann — whom Winquist brings together into a surprising and novel synthesis — Winquist interprets the Church as the community of the Word and positive theology as an explication of the Word. But unlike many other Protestant theologians of the Word, he grounds these theological affirmations on an incisive and creative philosophical analysis of language and of its creative role in human experience. And unlike many American interpreters of religious language, Winquist's analysis is transcendental and above all ontological, dependent not on the linguistic analytic tradition as much as it is on the interpretation of cognition in Bernard Lonergan and on the metaphysical analysis of language in Alfred North Whitehead.

This book is, therefore, first of all an exercise, and a profound one, in (1) a philosophical analysis of the role of language in creating new levels of experience and so of being; and (2) in phenomenological analysis of ordinary experience to uncover the "markings of transcendence" that undergird that experience — a preliminary enterprise that, following Karl Rahner, Winquist calls "foundational theology" as the analysis of the ontological role of religious language and so of the possibility of both Word and Church. Secondly, the book is an interpretation of (1) positive or dogmatic theology as the witness to the Word — where, as Winquist puts it, "the markings of transcendence of the boundary move into the range of meaningful experience" — and so (2) of the Church as the community where the Word-event, the witness of language to the appearance of transcendence takes place and is creative of new levels of life. Language, Winquist has told us, mediates between actualities and possibilities in experience; thus eschatological language, central to the witness of the Church, mediates ultimate possibility into the dreary and warped actualities of our life and, like all important language, opens up new possibilities of consciousness and of being to its community and its world. As these brief remarks show, Winquist is careful not to let the prior philosophical prolegomenon determine the content of proclamation but only to allow it to illumine for us the role of the Word in its possibility, its necessity for our fullest experience, and its creativity in opening us to new possibilities. I know of no work in the most recent American theology that so fruitfully combines philosophical insight and theological understanding to open up for us at the deepest level the role of symbol, proclamation and Church in the context of modern life.

Langdon Gilkey

December 30, 1974
University of Chicago

CHAPTER I

RELIGION AND THE CRISIS OF MEANING

I

he achievement of modern consciousness has been identified with
the destruction of illusion and the transcendence of mythology. Religion
has been displaced from the center of contemporary culture. The vision of
hope and the affirmation of human dignity have been translated into
languages of secular understanding. New images of self realization have
emerged against a background of relative meanings and provisional horizons. The consciousness of reality and intelligibility have been narrowed
and separated from the demands of historical consciousness to facilitate
clear and distinct understanding and expedite technical advance.

The renewed interest in the study of religion confronts a crisis of
meaning when it tries to comprehend the primary significance of the
primitive and classical mythic structures that are deeply rooted in the life
and thought of past cultures. Religious discourse is no longer meaningful
in everyday experience because it introduces a concern for meaning that
extends beyond the range of secular consciousness. The recognition of
the disconnectedness of modern experience from archaic sensitivities to
what is real and important has come to reflect a dimension of poverty
rather than illuminate a mark of achievement in modern life.

The inheritance of meaning and revelation of depth in human experience that have traditionally nourished the growth of religious communities through embodiment in ritual, mythology and confessions of
faith are denied their importance by the eclipse of religious discourse.
The shadow of meaninglessness has fallen on the life of the church
because its theological self consciousness has become increasingly isolated from the realities of immediate experience. The recovery of meaning is the first task of theology. The theologian must urgently explore the
experiential foundations of religious discourse and mythic-symbolic language and enable us to receive the grant of language that has been carefully passed down to us through generations of experience.

We cannot simply say that we have lost the meaning of past mythologies and correct our oversight through a review of past cultures. The relationship of man to myth in the present age is best characterized by a forgetfulness of the experience that is expressed in the achievement of mythological understanding.[1] The restoration of mythological understanding requires a recovery of experience at the edge of language that exceeds secular anticipations of meaning. Mythic-symbolic language has traditionally provided a voice for experiences of depth and need that have been moved to the periphery of modern consciousness. Even death, life's common denominator, is pushed to the edges of our shared life except when it disrupts the business of everyday concerns. Death is often individualized and denied its communal significance. The valuation of continuity in the community's life supercedes the experience of reality and justifies the forgetfulness of meaning. As in this example, the secularization of consciousness is a function of reductionism.

In traditional understanding, mythic-symbolic language preserves a relationship to sacred realities. Times, places, people, or events were sacred because they manifested themselves as wholly different from the realities of everyday experience.[2] The horizons of traditional experience extended beyond the confines of ordinary expectations and provided a background for the appearance of extraordinary happenings. Consciousness of the sacred was nourished by the discontinuities of life, the appearance of anomalies, and the emergence of novel actualizations. The appreciation for dimensions of otherness in the vision of the sacred could be transmitted only through a language that admitted irregularity and a multiplicity of meanings. The multivalence of mythic-symbolic language expresses dimensions of depth in experience but retards the achievements of systematic thinking. The commitment of modern thought to precision, clarity and an economy of language naturally sought a language of univocal expression. The secularization of experience narrowed the horizons of understanding to realize provisional goals and eliminate the prohibitive complications of multivalent expression. The desacralization of the cosmos is a sacrifice of modern thought for the security of technological growth and the clarity of objective understanding.

The substitution of scientific paradigms for mythological paradigms in the determination of meaning has radically altered our sense of reality. The gain in clarity and precision was accompanied by a loss of depth in perceptive awareness. The wide range of experiences unified through the symbolic use of language has been reduced to one frame of reference and the singularity of experience has been substituted for the unification of experience. The experience is significantly altered because it is no longer a coming together. The descriptive use of language is not conceived as a creative act. The language gain is a function of clarity and no longer directed toward the enlargement of experience. The cost for precision in intellectual growth has been the restriction of experience to the commonplace. Certainly the detailed analysis of ordinary experience has surprised us in its microscopic complexity. In fact, revolutions in scientific understanding have called into question the simplicity of our method and understanding of the intellectual task. However, it is the loss of meaning that has come to overshadow our accomplishments that really underlies new reflections on the role of mythic-symbolic language in the shaping of our cultural vision.

Can any culture really be free from the mythic function of language without a loss of meaning and importance?[3] The readiness of theology to follow the cultural movement toward secularization brings this question into the life of the church. Can a religious community sustain the depth of its fellowship devoid of mythic-symbolic language? The inability of contemporary theology to talk meaningfully of God in the language of secularity suggests that we cannot dispense with religious language without a loss of vitality. Instead, theologians talk about the task of theology because the loss of a meaningful language has issued forth in a vocational crisis that has uprooted the place of the theologian in the life of the church. Bernard Meland's claim that "myth implies discernment which arises from involvement" would now suggest that the loss of myth is accompanied by a loss of meaningful involvement.[4] Examining the mythic-symbolic function of language is not merely a reflection on the possibility for religious discourse, but it is also the foundation for new reflections on the complexity of our life together and the meaning of the church. The crisis of meaning is a crisis at the center of communal life.

The definition of ministry is also reconstructed in the context of foundational inquiry. The discernment of meaning and the recovery of possibility in mythic-symbolic consciousness opens the way for a reconciliation with the visions and achievements of past cultures that can be carried forward in a future realization. Myth deepens the sensitivity for a ministry that refuses to be conformed to the expectations of the moment. The boundaries of everydayness cease to be the acceptable limits of intelligibility in a ministry that refuses to affirm that life has no depth and that extraordinary experiences have no meaning. A language of multiple meanings is required to articulate and sustain the refusal to live solely on the surface of experience. Thus, mythic-symbolic language is revalorized in the emergence of ministries that can live on many levels of experience and meaning. Myth is returned to its primary function of disclosure in an active ministry.

The crisis of meaning in contemporary religious thought is probably best illustrated by examining what it means to return myth to its primary function. The importance of mythology in primitive and traditional thought cannot be understood if it is equated with disguise. Even as a mask of God the primary function of mythic-symbolic language has been to reveal otherwise hidden dimensions of reality. To not be able to view a mask of God was not to be able to view God at all. The mythological masks of God are not false perceptions but they are the possibility for seeing God. Modern attempts to unmask God result only in a loss of perception and a loss of meaning.

A distinction was made between myths and fables in primitive and traditional societies. The myth was a true story that reveals the structure of reality.[5] By narrating a sacred history or true story, the myth discloses the possibilities for being in the world. The myth is a revelatory paradigm for all significant human activities.[6] The real, the powerful, and the sacred are equated and the myth tells the story of reality, power, and sacrality. In contemporary thought, experience cannot be valued because of its power or reality because there is no longer a vehicle for this evaluation. What is clear and distinct may not be real, powerful and sacred, and more importantly what is real, powerful and sacred may not be clear and distinct. The crisis of meaning in modern cluture appears when meaning is a valuation allied with reality rather than with clarity. Then the economy of language fails to articulate or enhance experience.

The symbols of Christianity are not an exception. They have lost their efficacy in the conscious experience of modern man because of the secularization of understanding and the assignment of meaning to clarity of thought rather than to the reality of experience. The extraordinary affirmation that Jesus was the Christ rooted in the community's vision of reality and existential power is disqualified in modern thought by requirements of historical credibility ascertained by the clear and distinct judgments of scholarship. The success of scholarship has not recovered the power of Christian symbols. The loss of viability arises from an alteration in the meaning of meaning. In fact, it is the achievement of modern textual scholarship that has shifted the focus of hermeneutics toward the question of meaning itself. We now realize that to understand the confession of faith in the early Christian church it is not enough to know what was said. Textual scholarship is only a beginning phase of hermeneutics. The determination of historical meanings does not exhaust the question of meaning. The question of meaning is an existential question that must be worked through the experience of every culture if meaning is to be conjoined with reality. The hermeneutical question is basically the question as to whether there are areas of experience in our lives that can convey an enlarged sense of reality and restore meaning to religious concepts.

The restoration of symbolic language and even understanding the symbols in a confession of faith require an interpretation that can draw upon the fullness of experience. This interpretation is an enlargement rather than a reduction of experience. Instead of unmasking mythology we now see the need for interpretation that respects the original enigma of symbols.[7]

A fullness of language is given in symbolism but how do we relate to this grant of meaning in contemporary theology? It is impossible to return to a naive belief in mythology that identifies the *true stories* of mythology with history.[8] Interpretation is the possibility for an ongoing participation in the meaning of mythic-symbolic language but we are still faced with the problem of entering into the aura of power and meaning surrounding mythology that gives interpretation its existential significance. Paul Ricoeur sees a circularity in the hermeneutical problem. "We must understand in order to believe, but we must believe in order to understand."[9] Uncritical belief is no longer possible. Thus, we need a valuation of mythic-symbolic language that approximates the significance of belief but which does not naively identify mythology with historical or scientific explanation. That is, we need to believe in the importance of the mythological function even if we cannot identify with the content of specific mythologies. This opens the hermeneutical circle to modern experience and returns to mythology an active voice in human affairs. The interpretative power of mythic-symbolic language is thereby introduced into the deliberations of modern consciousness without a reduction of its existential function. A new dimension of meaning is opened for our shared experience.

II

Thus, it is my intention in this book to address the crisis of meaning in theology by a foundational analysis of mythic-symbolic language and an interpretation of the functions of ministry and community in their relationship to the importance of the hermeneutical circle. I hope that with greater insight into the functioning of language we can better understand the importance of a ministry of proclamation that can lead the fellowship of the church toward a deeper level of meaning and satisfaction. I begin my formal inquiry with the recognition that there is a crisis of meaning in Christianity that has brought the church to a silence concerning the fullness of its mission. Examining the complex of themes in the relationship between word and sacrament I try to recover some of the basic features characteristic of mythic-symbolic language.

Distinctions are drawn between analyses of the act and content of word usage that suggest a reformulation of the theological task. In particular, the ontological significance of language is subject to a transcendental analysis of the possibility for the word-event. This is the foundational specialty that secures entrance into the hermeneutical circle. It is metaphysically prior to the dogmatic formulations of theology that can be shaped from within the hermeneutical circle.

Foundational theology does not begin with the content of faith. It is concerned with the analysis of the structure of the word-event and takes as its starting point the subjectivity of experience. The consciousness of self is the reality principle in the development of a foundational theology. Foundational theology is concerned with the primacy of action in the dialectical relationship between the act and content of knowing. The specific contents of conceptual achievement are transcended by the fullness of action. New questions can always be raised concerning the adequacy of understanding. This elementary transcendence moves thinking toward an increasingly larger horizon of understanding. No artificial restriction can be placed on this dialectical movement for there are no limitations that are unquestionable. This means that the horizon of foundational theology is unrestricted. That is, the focus of foundational theology is on the structure and possibility for the act of knowing which is virtually unrestricted. The unconditional horizon under which foundational theology develops can be no less than the horizon of being itself. Thus, there is an undefined relationship between foundational theology and metaphysics. Metaphysics is used to help uncover ontological relationships and meanings resident in the act of knowing.

A philosophical interpretation of hermeneutics is within the proper range of inquiry in foundational theology. Metaphysical categories are used to explore dimensions of subjectivity. This does not mean that foundational theology is identical with metaphysical inquiry. In this work, metaphysical categories are viewed as heuristic structures used by reflective thinking in its increasing self consciousness. This is what I will mean when I say that hermeneutics is allied with metaphysics but is not reducible to metaphysics. Foundational theology is in all of its workings a preliminary inquiry in preparation for the way of symbolic thinking.

Foundational theology uses metaphysics to illuminate a diversity of language functions that in turn implies the need for many levels of interpretation in a fully developed hermeneutic. Philosophy serves theology by extending the range of meaning and experience. But meaning is a concrete achievement of dialectical action and foundational inquiry naturally passes into a second phase of inquiry using a phenomenological method. The elaboration of meaning is bound to the recollection of being, but the manifestations of meaning are visible only as experience comes into consciousness. The second phase of foundational theology seeks to determine how we can see or hear the ontological meanings which dwell in conscious meanings. Thus, I extend the elementary structural analysis of transcendence into recognizable regions of concrete experience by the construction of a topographical model using material from the history of religions, literary criticism, and the social sciences. It is my suggestion that the interpretation of universal human themes associated with and revealed in birth, puberty, love, marriage, death, boredom, meaninglessness, hope and vision move man to the frontiers of understanding and even unsophisticated thinkers must draw upon images of depth and transcendence to render these experiences intelligible.

The topography is not an attempt to rescue religion from secularism as much as it is an attempt to rescue experience from obscurity. Important regions of experience are often pushed aside because they are not clean well lighted places. Language is not confined to one meaning in these places. Some conscious situations mirror the ambiguity and ambivalence of meanings that are resident in the dialectic of actuality and possibility on the level of ontological passage. It is possible for any experience to mirror its ontological foundations, but there are in every epoch some experiences which are more easily deciphered. These experiences clearly bear witness to their complicity with transcendence. In the phenomenological development of the topography I survey seven regions of experiencing which are marked by an ambiguity of levels of meaning because they express characteristics of their ontological foundation in their concrete realization. Paul Ricoeur refers to three of these areas, the cosmic, oneiric, and poetic, as zones of the emergence of symbolism.[10] To these regions I have added comic, ludic, neurotic, and dramatic dimensions of experience. The evaluation of these regions of meaning requires a complex view of self determination that recognizes the meaning of transcendence. However, I intend to show that the meaning of transcendence escapes the categories of secular understanding. The phenomenological analysis in the topography does not come to a completion. Because the topography raises questions of meaning that it cannot answer, it puts us underway toward a larger horizon.

The topography opens the hermeneutical circle to secular culture. It ascertains the significance of transcendence without being an understanding of transcendence. The topography shows that there is a reason to listen for the word of God. Thus, the preliminary reflections of foundational theology prepare the way for the hermeneutic of the word of God. Positive theology begins with the certainty that the word of God has entered language. The central symbol that initiates a positive Christian theology is given in the confession of the community that Jesus is the Christ. That is, the Christ-event is symbolic and gives rise to thought. Thus, we can talk about the hermeneutic power of the word of God.

Theology develops beyond the foundational analysis of secular experience because of the interpretative power of the word of God. In fact, the topography is transformed by interpretation within the hermeneutical circle. This does not mean that we can return to a precritical reading of the

Bible. The hermeneutic of the word of God is valorized by reflections in foundational theology because its meaning is greatly expanded by the dialectical conception of a word-event and a pattern of application is discerned in the topography of sacred markings. Foundational theology and dogmatic theology are conjoined in contemporary thought for a reinterpretation of the responsibilities of Christian mission and life.

The final chapters of this book explore the meaning of Christian ministry and the concept of community using tools and insights developed in foundational theology. These reflections speak from within the hermeneutical circle and expand the chapter on the hermeneutic of the word of God. However, the interpretative power of the word of God cannot be isolated in a sanctuary. It is directed toward the world and is given a historical embodiment. Actually the movement into the hermeneutical circle is a deep involvement with the world. The ecclesial mystery in the fellowship of disciples is a disclosure of worldly possibilities. In the communion of possibility the world transcends its secular achievements, but never ceases to be itself. The hermeneutic of the word of God reveals the disparity between secularity and reality, and it refuses to let go of reality.

Thus, it is the argument of this book that by beginning with the problem of meaninglessness theology can enter into a meaningful dialogue with contemporary culture. The questions that are addressed to theology are questions that are addressed to the culture as a whole. By exploring its own foundations, theology opens a new dimension of understanding for the full range of experience. Theology secures its place in the modern world by sharing in the search for meaning.

NOTES

1. Paul Ricoeur, *The Symbolism of Evil* (New York: Harper & Row, 1967), p. 349.
2. Mircea Eliade, *The Sacred and the Profane* (New York: Harper Torchbooks, 1961), p. 11.
3. Bernard Meland, *Faith and Culture* (London: Allen and Unwin, 1955), p. 26.
4. *Ibid.*, p. 44.
5. Mircea Eliade, *Myths, Dreams and Mysteries* (New York: Harper Torchbooks, 1967), p. 15; Mircea Eliade, *Myth and Reality* (New York: Harper Torchbooks, 1968), p. 1.
6. Eliade, *Myth and Reality*, p. 8.
7. Ricoeur, *The Symbolism of Evil*, p. 349.
8. *Ibid.*, p. 351.
9. Ibid., p. 351; Paul Ricoeur, *Freud and Philosophy: An Essay in Interpretation* (New Haven: Yale University Press, 1970), p. 28.
10. Ricoeur, *Freud and Philosophy*, pp. 14-15.

CHAPTER II

THE SACRAMENT OF
THE WORD OF GOD

I

here is wide-spread recognition that the articulation of the Christian faith has become problematic within Christian communities. The importance and force of preaching have become unintelligible even to its users. The crisis faced by the church is that it is no longer able to translate the fullness of the Christian gospel into the concrete experience of its contemporary communities. The despair of the preacher and the church over the loss of words through which expression can be given to the word of God has often brought the church to silence concerning its eschatological mission. Contemporary theology has the responsibility to revalorize the language of the gospel before it can become a useful servant of the modern church.

The loss of meaningful religious discourse throws theological inquiry back to foundational questions concerning the revelation of God in the history of Christianity. How is it possible to speak meaningfully of the revelation of God at all? The theologian can look at the work of historians of religions for some clues to understanding his own situation. When the theologian turns back to the historical revelation of God in Christ he needs to go beyond the historical task of piecing together the constellation of events which are associated with this revelation and explain the modality for the manifestation of the sacred which is disclosed in this revelation.[1] It is not enough to acknowledge that the Christ-event is a paradoxical coming together of God and man if we do not see in this revelation a structure for the continuing manifestation of the sacred which makes a claim upon man's posture toward existence. The coming together of God and man remains imbedded in a history which is unintelligible to us unless we can separate from the particularities of that historical situation structural elements which contribute to our understanding of the universal nature of the Christ-event.

The question concerning how it is possible to speak of the revelation of God is both historical and morphological. It includes inquiry into the structural elements which underlie the revelation of God. What are the structures which make possible the concrete manifestation of the sacred in the Christian community? This is not an irrelevant question for the concrete life of the church. Unless we can understand the modalities for the revelation of God in Jesus the Christ, the church cannot intelligibly talk about the continuing revelation of God in the church as the body of Christ. The notion of the incarnation claims concreteness and visibility for the love and will of God in the human community. But, what does the Christian church mean when it asserts that the *Word* was made flesh? How does the incarnation give visibility to the reality of God?

The concern to show how the sacred is concretely manifested is an attempt to discern an area of experience that restores meaning to basic theological notions. If Christianity is to have a future there must be a place where the sacred is manifested concretely in the life of the church.

There is no easy movement that can be made by the theologian which will disclose the structural foundation for the manifestation of the sacred in the Christian experience. We must begin by studying the experience of the church within its own frame of reference.[2] We remain within the broad range of Catholic and Protestant theology if we focus on the complex of themes associated with word and sacrament. I, however, would like to suggest that there is a primacy of the word and that we can best understand the real presence of the Christ within the life of the church by penetrating into the meaning of language and the significance of the word of God.

We can begin our discussion of word and sacrament with the concreteness of sacramentality since it is clearly illustrative of the church's concern with the continuing manifestation of the sacred. E. Schillebeeckx has suggested that "the sacraments are the properly human mode of encounter with God."[3]

Sacramental activity gives historical visibility to the redeeming love of God. Schillebeeckx claims that the life of Jesus is the primordial sacrament in the Christian experience. Divine love is made available in history through its transformation into a human form. Jesus' love is the expression of Divine love.[4] This corresponds to the phenomenological insight that the meaningful expression of a human intention toward another person requires an expressive word or gesture. Through the incarnation it becomes possible to talk about a Divine gesture and thus a Divine intention directed toward men.[5] The recognition that Jesus' love expresses Divine love locates the visibility of God's love for man in a particular historical situation. We can recognize in Jesus' love a manifestation of the sacred but it is very difficult to separate the essential modality for this manifestation of the sacred from the accidents in that particular historical situation until we turn to a confession of the resurrected Lord. A sacramental understanding of the Christian faith must include the resurrection story and thereby embody the confession that Jesus is the Christ. If we do not have an understanding of sacramentality that includes the resurrection, the encounter with God remains bound to a personal encounter with the man Jesus.[6] Jesus, however, is dead. A continuing manifestation of the sacred must include structures which go beyond the life of Jesus and incorporate the resurrection of the Christ. The structural foundation for the continuing manifestation of the sacred must account for a prolongation of the incarnation made possible by the resurrection witness. We look to the sacraments for a clue because of the claim that they are the earthly extension of the "body of the Lord."[7].

The traditional division which is made in sacramental theology between the matter and form of a sacrament is an attempt to understand the structures which underlie sacramental activity. This distinction usually favors the importance of the liturgical word in a sacramental activity. For example, Augustine has said that "A word comes to an element and a sacrament is there."[8] The word of God is a foundational concept for grasping the efficacy of the sacraments.

If we were to begin with an examination of the elements or matter of sacramental activity it would soon be very clear that in themselves they would have no efficacy. Like any other part of the world they have the potentiality for participation in the manifestation of the sacred. As Eliade notes in *Patterns in Comparative Religion*, "anything man has ever handled, felt, come in contact with or loved can become a hierophany."[9] Becoming hierophanous means that the element is an aspect of a modality for the manifestation of the sacred. The element is not itself a manifestation of the sacred. The matter or elements of sacramental life remain secular or profane except as they belong to a hierophanous act.

Since the sacramental elements remain secular before the examining eye they do not explain the fruitfulness of sacramental life. We are inclined to ask what Augustine meant by his claim that when the word comes to the element the sacrament is there. What does the word bring to the elements?

We will not be able to understand the meaning of a sacramental life until we are able to understand the role of the word of God in sacramental activity. The sacramental understanding of the continuing revelation of God focuses attention on the meaning of the word of God. We are still asking how God continues to be visible in history. We are still asking about the meaning of the resurrection for the continuing life of the church.

The importance of the sacraments is intertwined with the meaning of the resurrection accounts. In summarizing his reflections on the fruitfulness of the sacraments in the church Schillebeeckx says, "It is by the sacraments that we journey toward our final goal — the sacramental way is our hidden road to Emmaus, on which we are accompanied by our Lord."[10]

The recognition of the Christ as portrayed in the Emmaus road account of the resurrection reinforces the emphasis on the word of God as the key to understanding the continuing manifestation of the sacred in the church.

The two disciples are on the road to Emmaus and they are discussing matters which they did not understand. They were saddened because the visibility of God's love had been withdrawn from their experience. As they were walking a stranger (Jesus, who remained unrecognized) approached them and asked what they were discussing. They told the stranger about the immediate events associated with the crucifixion of Jesus and their disappointed hopes concerning the liberation of Israel. The stranger reviewed the scriptures concerning the Christ for the disciples. When they reached the village he went in to stay with them. "And when he sat down at table, he took bread and said the blessing; he broke the bread and offered it to them. Then their eyes were opened, and they recognized him. . . . They said to one another, 'Did we not feel our hearts on fire as he talked with us on the road and explained the scriptures to us?' "[11]

In this account, the visibility of the sacred lies in the appearance of the crucified Jesus. The sacred manifests itself in the company of disciples through the resurrected Christ. The basis of faith is not our encounter with the historical Jesus. If an emphasis on a personal savior is interpreted to mean that the Christian faith is rooted in a personal relationship to the historical Jesus, then we have learned nothing from the experience of the disciples on the road to Emmaus.

The disciples' experience was not that of a personal relationship with the historical Jesus. They met a stranger who interpreted the scriptures for them. They felt their hearts on fire as they were hearers of the word of God. They were still relating to a stranger. When their eyes were opened and they recognized the risen Christ, he disappeared. The experience was rooted in the hearing of the word of God.

The Emmaus road experience of the resurrected Christ is a paradigm for understanding the sacraments. The Christ-event is the primordial sacrament of the encounter with God. The word of God is given visibility through the Christ-event; and, the Christ-event is given sacramental visibility through the word of God as it is brought to a historical situation. In the Emmaus road legend the stranger sat down at table with the disciples; he took bread and blessed it; he broke the bread and offered it to them before their eyes were opened. According to this account, the stranger was recognized as the resurrected Christ at the breaking of the bread. The sacramental elements are here present in such a way that this resurrection account should be viewed as a prototype for the church's continuing participation in the Eucharist.

This, of course, calls into question the institution of the Eucharist as it is usually presented in the New Testament and Catholic liturgy. Johannes Betz writes in *Sacramentum Mundi* that a radical circle in Protestant theology traces the institution of the sacrament to the early church's understanding of itself. He says that it is their claim that "The historical fact from the life of the Lord in connection with the Eucharist is simply his fellowship at table with his disciples and sinners, which he understood as an anticipation of the eschatological community."[12]

The Emmaus road story tells of the table fellowship of the resurrected Christ with his disciples. This Eucharistic legend is not dependent on the life of the historical Jesus. This table fellowship depends only upon the presence of the word of God and it is not subject to the particularities of history. This prototype for the Eucharist takes place in the "eternal now." The Eucharist is central to the continuing life of the church because it is not limited to a special historical situation. The Eucharist is constituted by the presence of the word of God. Here the word of God is primary. It is the modality for the continuing manifestation of the sacred. Thus, we learn from the Emmaus road account of the resurrection that table fellowship can be sacramental because there is a real presence of the Christ wherever there is a coming together for a speaking and hearing of the word of God. We again affirm that the resurrected Lord is present to the Christian community through his word. The importance of preaching in the sacramental life is that the Christ is present in the interpretation and proclamation of the gospel.[13]

II

The problem with which we began our inquiry appears to have even greater significance. The word is a modality for the manifestation of the sacred, but the language of faith has become unintelligible even to many of its users. A concept of the word must be lifted out of the confusions associated with the unintelligibility of religious discourse.

Some theologians and preachers have come to admit that in the expression of the Christian faith they don't know their way about. They fail to understand the meaning of the gospel because they do not command a clear view of the *use* of their words. As Wittgenstein has noted, these questions have the form of philosophical problems.[14] We need to examine what it means to *use* religious language before we continue our inquiry into the word as a modality for the manifestation of the sacred.

Analytical philosophers have carefully examined the use of words and their insights are important for the theologian. Wittgenstein would deny that there is a single essence to language which could help the theologian come to a self-understanding of his task.[15] He says that the similarity in appearance of words in print is deceiving to us because it lends credibility to the position that there is a basic unity between the words in our language or a single essence to language. What we fail to see in this appearance of words is the diversity of applications with which they are associated.[16]

One of the most interesting analogies that Wittgenstein used to illumine the functional meaning of words was a comparison of words with pieces in a chess game. A chess piece does not have a single meaning for the game of chess, and, although we may learn a simple definition of the basic moves which are possible for this piece in isolation from an actual game of chess, this is only the beginning of the activity in which that piece finds its meaning. The chess piece can never be given an essential definition. It is only when we learn about the game and practice it that we begin to understand the family of meanings to which the chess piece is related.[17] To complete this analogy, we realize that to understand a word we must go to the situations in which the word is spoken. This means that it is not the theologian's task to determine absolute meanings for words used in religious discourse. He is not seeking for an ideal religious language which can invariably and unambiguously give expression to the Christian gospel.

Part of the confusion in contemporary theology is that we have not understood the function of words and language in religious discourse. I wish to acknowledge the correctness of Wittgenstein's claim that in a large number of cases the meaning of a word is its *use* in language, but I wish also to make a much more radical statement and suggest that the meaning of language is its *use* in life.

Man is situated in the world and it is impossible to talk about the situations in which a word is used without entering the world of lived space and time. To talk about the use of words in language requires that we also talk about the use of language in man's lived experiences. The establishment of paradigm cases for the use of words in the context of the life-world requires a phenomenological method which does not exclude any uses of language. It is not at all clear that language is used similarly in every situation.

Before we can understand the religious use of language we will have to examine the situations in which language is used religiously. What are the functions of words in those situations in which language is properly called religious language? This incorporates the question concerning how language can be a dynamic element in sacramental activity. How does language function so that the resurrected Christ is visible to the disciples on the Emmaus road?

Language is multivalent. It is imbedded in the human situation in more than one way. To understand the specific meanings and functions of language we must turn to the many situations to which it belongs and to the many uses it has in these situations.

The use of paradigm cases describing the function of language in our ordinary experience can be a useful tool for exploring the uncharted uses of language, but we must not use these paradigm cases to exclude from our vision the broad variety of meanings rooted in the multifunctional character of language. The major task is to understand the extraordinary use of the sacramental word.

In the everydayness of our lives it is clear that there are at least two very different uses for language. Language points and language carries. Language has ostensive and descriptive functions. Language can transport and transform the user. Paradigm cases should be developed which illuminate both functions of language but they should be understood only as being heuristic structures used hermeneutically to elicit from the fullness of language its meanings in specific situations. It cannot be claimed a priori that these are the only functions for language. We must always take care not to destroy nuances of meaning belonging to the intricacies of human relationships for the sake of methodological simplicity.

The descriptive function of language has been thoroughly documented in contemporary philosophical thought. In fact, the positivist's concern with empirical verification is a recognition that language can point to empirically observable situations and thereby function descriptively. In teaching a language we often point to the objects or actions to which the words refer. In the everydayness of our experience the ostensive and descriptive functions of language are very important. A. J. Ayer's verifiability principle in *Language, Truth and Logic* is a helpful notion when we are examining the ostensive and descriptive functions of language. When Ayer says "that a sentence is factually significant to any given person, if, and only if, he knows how to verify the proposition which it purports to express," he has delineated one of the functions of language.[18] Clear thinking is simply the matter of putting before us the empirical situation which our propositions purport to describe. When there is no empirical referent for our propositions, then they do not function descriptively or ostensively.

The movement away from positivism in the analytical tradition in philosophy suggests that Ayer's verifiability principle defined too restrictively the function of language. Wittgenstein suggested in his *Philosophical Investigations* that "There are countless kinds: countless different kinds of use of what we call 'symbols,' 'words,' 'sentences.'"

And this multiplicity is not something fixed, given once for all; but new types of language, new language-games, as we may say, come into existence, and others become obsolete and get forgotten. Here the term 'language-game' is meant to bring into prominence the fact that the speaking of language is part of an activity or a form of life."[19] Wittgenstein provides the raw material for a transition to nondescriptive and nonostensive functions of language. This is a movement which he is not inclined to make. Very interestingly he says that "philosophical problems arise when language *goes on holiday*."[20] He defines the philosophical task as bringing words back from their metaphysical to their everyday uses.[21] Thus, he does not help us to penetrate into the extraordinary times when language goes on holiday that are of such interest to the theologian and historian of religions. What does it mean when language is used metaphysically or when language is used sacramentally? How do we understand Heidegger's claim that "It is in words and language that things first come into being and are."[22] Language can be creative. It can transform situations.

We do not need to go to extraordinary situations to find examples of the non-descriptive functions of language. For instance, in the everydayness of our experiences we see language used to transform casual relationships into intimate situations. The language of seduction or the honest expression of love are seldom descriptive of empirically observable situations. Quite often the language aims at a future realization. It is a lure which transforms the character of a relationship. The function of the language is to carry the speaker and the hearer to new regions of experience. It would violate the intimate situation, distort the function of language which is determined by the situation, and embarrass the speaker if we were to ask what is meant by the statement "I love you." We could well expect that the speaker's response would be ambiguous and even meaningless if language could only function ostensively and descriptively. "I love you" makes a claim upon the situation in which it is spoken and creates new possibilities for a future relationship. The intent of the language is to transform a situation instead of describe a situation. We may wish to say that the language functions ontologically. It contributes to the way in which a man sits in the world.

The examination of the religious use of language more clearly reveals the ontological function of language. This can be demonstrated in the examination of mythic structures or theological affirmations.

The fact that theological language is not merely descriptive or ostensive is seen in the elusive search for the historical Jesus and in the radical theologians unusual claim that the historical Jesus is Lord.[23] If theological language describes or merely points to the life of the historical Jesus, how does it make a claim upon the life of contemporary man?

There is the serious problem that not much can be known about the life of the historical Jesus and what is known has the form of historical knowledge. We can only encounter the historical Jesus as we would any other figure from the past. The problem is compounded by the fact that we cannot encounter Jesus as if he were a figure from the past who was privileged to have a sensitive biographer. Bultmann said that "we can, strictly speaking, know nothing of the personality of Jesus."[24] Thus, no appeal to Jesus' personality can make a claim upon our lives. It stretches our knowledge to talk about the life of the historical Jesus as a moral paradigm. With all of these limitations it is hard to understand what the radical theologian means when he says that the historical Jesus is Lord in our secular society. When religious discourse is only a pointing at the life of the historical Jesus, it is no longer efficacious.

This impotency of the descriptive function of religious language can be contrasted with the neo-orthodox claim that we can existentially confront the risen Lord present through the word of God. This existential confrontation does not issue from a pointing toward the historical events surrounding the resurrection accounts. If we are to speak of the efficacy of the word of God, we are not talking about the descriptive and ostensive functioning of language. Existential confrontation implies active response. The legend of the Emmaus road account of the resurrection reinforces the need for an understanding of a language function which can account for the transformation of a situation. The disciples' eyes were opened. They felt their hearts on fire as they listened to the word of God. The speaking and hearing of the word of God basically does not have an explanatory function. The word of God disclosed the identity of the stranger. The speaking of the word of God is not as much associated with description and explanation as it is with disclosure, illumination, and transformation.

This nondescriptive functioning of religious language is also evidenced by the irreducible symbolic character of myth. Both theologians and historians of religions have suggested that there is an existential value to religious symbolism. (Of course, this does not preclude a complementary descriptive or ostensive function for religious symbols.) For example, Tillich saw that a symbol can open up levels of reality which are otherwise closed to us and it can also unlock elements in our own soul which echo these deeper levels of reality.[25] Religious symbols have given expression to the otherwise inexpressable paradoxical union of conditional existence and unconditional reality. Even if we don't know what these symbols mean they represent language-events which require our full attention if we are to understand their function. Ricoeur notes that symbolic signs are opaque and he even suggests that "this opaqueness is the symbol's very profundity, an inexhaustible depth."[26] Myth and symbol are not used for explanation. Myth, when it is allowed to function as myth, is not an explanatory system; but, it is an opening up and manifestation of a primordial situation.[27]

Eliade has also suggested in several essays that symbols have an existential function.[28] He says that it is the existential dimension of religious symbols which distinguish them from concepts which merely have an explanatory function. "Thanks to the symbol, the individual experience is 'awoken' and transmuted into a spiritual act."[29] The function of religious symbolism cannot possibly be reduced to description. Eliade expands his insight into the function of symbols through depth psychology. Symbols speak to the whole person. He says, "Depth psychology has taught us that the symbol delivers its message and fulfills its *function* even when its meaning escapes awareness."[30]

If a symbol can fulfill its function even when the meaning of the symbol escapes awareness or if the symbol can deliver its message even though we are not aware of the message, it appears that the importance of symbolism cannot be understood by a descriptive theory of language. The message of the symbol is not what is usually meant by a "message." A precise explanatory proposition cannot be substituted for a symbol if the message of the symbol is to be delivered.

The religious use of language depends upon an ontological understanding of the functioning of language. The power of language to create new situations or carry men to new regions of experience explains why language can become a modality for the manifestation of the sacred. Language brings to the sacraments a vitality because the speaking and hearing of the word of God is basically an act of being and not merely a description of an ontological act.

It would be premature to say how language is to be understood as a modality for the manifestation of the sacred within a context of sacramentality. We can, however, begin to see that sacramental theology cannot be separated from a theology of the word. The word-event brings the reality of God into the historical experience of the church and is therefore essential to sacramentality. On the other hand, the word-event is always imbedded in the particularities of history and therefore cannot be seen or understood as isolated from sacramentality. The speaking of the word of God and every other hierophany are historical events and must be understood in relation to history.[31] Just as an examination of the sacramental elements used in the Christian church yields no meaning without the presence of a word-event, the word-event without historical embodiment is empty.

The sacramentality of speaking and hearing the word of God can explain the continuing presence of the incarnation in the church. This means that both the theological articulation of the Christian faith and phenomenological studies of Christian experience must investigate the fundamental relationship between sacramentality and the word-event if they are speaking to or about the living church.

III

Our insight into the multifunctional character of language suggests a reformulation of the theological task. Theological investigations can proceed on different levels which correspond with different language functions. For example, the relationship between word-event and sacrament can be approached through ontological inquiry into the nature of language or through a systematic examination of theological traditions. These are complementary concerns which should illuminate each other. In fact, these concerns define an important division of labor within theology which has too often been confused with the division between alternative theological positions.

There is a need for the complementary use of foundational and dogmatic theology. In accordance with the distinctions which have been noted, dogmatic theology is concerned with the systematic expression of Christian belief and foundational theology is concerned with fundamental questions about the possibility of theological understanding, the ontological status of the word-event, and the morphology of revelation.[32] Foundational theology is not bound to the specific content of any dogmatic theology. Foundational theology should come first because it permits the theologian to examine the word-event as a basic modality for the manifestation of the sacred without the restrictions of any particular theological tradition. Dogmatic theology can then complement foundational theology by showing how the word-event is imbedded in a specific historical situation.

To thoroughly develop a theology of word and sacrament, the dialectical relationship between the act and content of knowing must not be impeded by too hastily constructed formulations in either dogmatic or foundational theology. The act and content of the word-event function together and jointly constitute the possibility for the revelation of God within the continuing life of the church.

The conjunction of dogmatic and foundational theology directs inquiry into both the nature of language and the understanding which is possible through language. Dogmatic theology turns to the hermeneutic function of the word itself.[33] There is a legacy, inheritance or grant of meaning given to man through language. The ontological significance of language justifies Heidegger's claim that language is the house of Being.[34] The dogmatic theologian journeys into realms of experience which are opened to him through the grant of language. The meaning of the word-event can be clearly elaborated, however, only when it is placed in the context of the life-world and understood as act.

Thus an outline of the present theological task includes investigation into the ontological status of the word-event and the development of a two-fold hermeneutic. An ontological understanding of the word-event is a necessary part of foundational theology. We need to understand the function of word-events in the configurations of human experience before we can thoroughly assess the importance of specific word usage. Thus, an ontological view of language initiates the development of a theological hermeneutic.

The responsibilities of foundational theology are not completed with an investigation of the ontological significance of word-events. The religious uses of language are concrete occurances and it is the responsibility of foundational theology to determine the actual character of these experiences. The dominate mood of secularity in contemporary culture shadows the presence of word-events, especially speaking and hearing the word of God, so that it is necessary to develop a phenomenological hermeneutic of concrete experience to locate dimensions of religious meaning.[35] Meanings must be sought in relationship to lived experience which complement ontological structures. A phenomenological hermeneutic seeks to expand the range of meanings and uncover depths of experience which are religious in character. The resultant topography guides the dogmatic theologian through contours of meaning to those regions of experience where man listens for the word of God.

Foundational theology frees the theologian to address himself to the problems of dogmatic theology. The primary task of dogmatic theology is the interpretation of the word of God. The interpretation of the word of God is an *act* through which the sacred is made visible within the community. This is one of the reasons why we can properly talk about the sacrament of the word of God. Speaking and hearing the word of God lies beneath the sacramental activity of the church and it is itself a modality for the continuing presence of the revelation of God. This is not a new insight. The reformation principle of *sola scriptura* was a hermeneutic thesis which claimed that scripture has illuminating power and makes visible the presence of God to the community.[36] The word of God is the sacrament of the encounter with the reality of God.

NOTES

1. See Mircea Eliade, *Patterns in Comparative Religion* (Cleveland: World Publishing, Meridian Book, 1963), p. 5.
2. cf. Mircea Eliade, *Myths, Dreams and Mysteries* (New York: Harper Torchbook, 1967), p. 13.
3. E Schillebeeckx, *Christ the Sacrament of the Encounter with God* (New York: Sheed and Ward, 1963), p. 6.
4. *Ibid.*, pp. 15, 39.
5. *Ibid*, p. 76.
6. See *Ibid.*, p. 40.
7. Ibid., p. 41.
8. Quoted by Schillebeeckx, *Ibid.*, p. 92.
9. *Patterns in Comparative Religion*, p. 11.
10. Schillebeeckx, p. 222.
11. Luke 24: 30-32 (N.E.B.); See Hans Dieter Betz, "The Origin and Nature of Christian Faith According to the Emmaus Legend," *Interpretation*, Vol. XXIII, No. 1, January 1969, for a penetrating interpretation of the Emmaus Road account of the resurrection.
12. Karl Rahner *et al.*, ed., *Sacramentum Mundi*, Vol. 2 (New York: Herder and Herder, 1968), p. 257.

13. See Betz, pp. 40-41.
14. Wittgenstein says that, "A philosophical problem has the form: 'I don't know my way about.'" Ludwig Wittgenstein, *Philosophical Investigations* (Oxford: Basil Blackwell, 1967), p. 49.
15. Wittgenstein, p. 31.
16. *Ibid.*, p. 6.
17. *Ibid.*, pp. 47, 80.
18. A J. Ayer, *Language, Truth and Logic* (New York: Dover Publications, 1946), p. 35.
19. Wittgenstein, p. 11.
20. *Ibid.*, p. 19.
21. *Ibid.*, p. 48.
22. Martin Heidegger, *An Introduction to Metaphysics* (Garden City: Doubleday Anchor Book, 1961), p. 11.
23. See Langdon Gilkey, *Naming the Whirlwind: The Renewal of God-Language* (Indianapolis: Bobbs-Merrill, 1969), pp. 147-178, for a penetrating critique of radical theology and Gilkey's important evaluation of the centrality of God-language in theology.
24. Rudolph Bultmann, *Jesus and the Word* (New York: Charles Scribner's Sons, 1958), p. 9.
25. Paul Tillich, *Dynamics of Faith* (New York: Harper Torchbook, 1958), p. 42.
26. Paul Ricoeur, "The Hermeneutics of Symbols," *International Philosophical Quarterly*, Vol. II, No. 2, May 1962, p. 194.
27. Paul Ricoeur, *The Symbolism of Evil* (New York: Harper and Row, 1967), pp. 165, 350.
28. See Mircea Eliade, *The Two and the One* (New York: Harper Torchbooks, 1970), chpt. V; or, Mircea Eliade, "Some Methodological Remarks on Religious Symbolism," *The History of Religions*, ed. Eliade and Kitagawa (Chicago: University of Chicago Press, 1959).
29. *The Two and the One*, p. 207.
30. Italics mine, "Some Methodological Remarks on Religious Symbolism," p. 107.
31. See *Patterns in Comparative Religions*, p. 2 for the twofold significance of a hierophany.
32. See David Tracy, "Prolegomena to a Foundational Theology," *Criterion*, Vol. Nine, No. 1, Autumn 1969.
33. Gerhard Ebeling, *Word and Faith* (London: SCM Press, 1963), p. 318.
34. Martin Heidegger, *On the Way to Language* (New York: Harper and Row, 1971), p. 63.
35. Gilkey, pp. 234, 277, 279-281.
36. Ebeling, pp. 306-307.

CHAPTER III

THE WORD OF GOD
IN FOUNDATIONAL THEOLOGY

𝒯

I

he church in its struggle for definition, relevance, and meaning
must thematize and explicate its basic experiences of the revelation
of God. The primacy of the word of God in the on-going sacramentality of religious life defines the character of this program for
theological investigations. The word of God is both the object and
subject of theological inquiry. As the basic modality for the manifestation of the sacred within the Christian experience, the conception
of the word of God is the central problematic for understanding the
possibility of a Christian knowledge of God, but it is also the dynamic
center of proclamation in dogmatic theology. It is precisely because
the word of God is the center of proclamation in dogmatic theology
that it is the central problematic of foundational theology.

Foundational theology is concerned with the meaning and structure
of basic revelatory events. Foundational theology is directed toward
understanding the activity through which the sacred manifests itself.
Thus, it focuses on the characteristic structures of the *act* of hearing
the word of God since the word of God is the center of Christian life.

The integrity of the word of God as it is manifested to the
church is not being called into question by reflections in foundational
theology. For example, inquiry in foundational theology would not
preclude the claims of a neo-orthodox theologian such as Karl
Barth when in the opening of *Church Dogmatics* he says, ''Dogmatics
is an act of obedience which is certain in faith.''[1] He thinks that
dogmatic theology should refuse to discuss basic questions concerning
the existence of God or the reality of revelation.[2] Thus, any prolegomena to dogmatic theology must, according to neo-orthodoxy, be
grounded in dogmatic theology. The validity of dogmatic theology
cannot be ascertained by an external critique. This means that if
foundational theology complements the neo-orthodox conception of

dogmatic theology, foundational theology is not an apologetic aimed at the justification of Christian belief.

Of course, the definition of the contemporary theological task is not bound to traditional formulations. It is, however, foolish to quickly abandon the insights of earlier theological positions before we have understood their relevance for the contemporary situation. The neo-orthodox emphasis on the self-containment of dogmatic theology is an interpretation and response to the reformation insistence on justification by faith. That the validity of Christian belief (including its formulation in dogmatic theology) is not subject to external confirmation is an insight which must be incorporated into our definition of foundational theology if it is to be consistent with the content of Christian proclamation.

The question of validity is subsumed under the conception of faith. It is not philosophy, but the word of God which reveals the truth of faith. Luther strongly proclaimed that

the attempt to establish or defend divine order with human reason, unless that reason has previously been established and enlightened by faith, is just as futile as if I would throw light upon the sun with a lightless lantern, or rest a rock upon a reed.[3]

Now, as we plainly see, God deals with us in no other way than by His holy Word and the sacraments which are like signs or seals of His Word. The very first thing necessary, then, is faith in these words and signs; for when God speaks and gives signs man must firmly and whole-heartedly believe that what He says and signifies is true, so that we do not consider Him a liar or a trickster, but hold Him to be faithful and true.[4]

We are not contemporary with Luther and New Testament scholarship has importantly changed our conceptions of the scriptural witness to the word of God. But a major thrust in Luther's statements is that the validity of the word of God is ascertained by our experience of the word of God and not by historical or philosophical criticism. This is a claim of faith and it is not overturned by our modernity.

To begin with the recognition that dogmatic theology is not dependent upon foundational theology for its validity removes our inquiry from the controversy between neo-orthodoxy and liberalism over the role of philosophy in theology. Foundational theology is not concerned with validity of dogmatic theology and therefore does not appeal to philosophy or other disciplines to justify particular theological positions, neo-orthodox or liberal. Foundational theology does not endanger the integrity of dogmatic theology by constructing an alternative gospel.

However, a much more serious problem is confronting contemporary theology than the validity of its constructions. Foundational theology is concerned with the prior question of the meaningfulness of theology itself. This question is important for all theological traditions. The recognition that "we don't know our way about" does not mean that dogmatic theology is incoherent or that the theologians lack logical acumen. Foundational theology is inquiry into the nature of theological activity. What are the religious uses of language? What does it mean to reflect on the word of God? Is theology a modality for the manifestation of the sacred? How is theology related to the life of the church? How is theology related to the life of secularized man? These are questions which must be addressed if we are "to know our way about" in contemporary theology.

Foundational theology is a transcendental inquiry. It probes the human situation for the possibilities and meanings of dogmatic theology. Philosophy can be a ready ally of foundational theology without threatening the integrity of the word of God. The meaninglessness of dogmatic theology is not a problem internal to dogmatic theology but it involves the failure to see the connectedness between theological activity and the experience of our being in the world. Foundational theology must revalorize the theological task itself so that the proclamations of dogmatic theology can be willingly heard.

In the above sense foundational theology is an apologetic for the meaningfulness of theology, but it is not an apologetic for the validity of any particular theology. Foundation theology is primarily a hermeneutical tool used to disclose structures of relatedness at the base of theological inquiry. Thus, the hermeneutical task is here not understood to be the translation of primitive Christianity into a contemporary idiom, but it is understood to be the unveiling of ontological structures which give existential importance to the religious use of language.[5] Within the corresponding scope of concrete experiencing, foundational theology must also define loci for the religious use of language.

II

The very different religious uses of language define layers of inquiry for foundational theology. On the most fundamental level, the use of language can be examined as an activity. On this level the important considerations focus on the ontological structures which make the religious use of language possible. The diverse contents for the religious uses of language are only of subsidiary interest for this inquiry. The fundamental context for language usage is the life-world. Analysis of language usage is on this level the analysis of structures which constitute the linguisticality of our being in the world. Being in the world is the context which illumines religious meanings and thereby initiates the hermeneutical endeavor.

The insight of post-Kantian philosophers that the structures of our being in the world are dynamic and formal gives further definition to foundational theology. That is, there are structures which are regulative of the content of objective knowledge and there are structures which are regulative of the act of knowing. The act of knowing is primary and transcends any specific content. The structures may well be identical but a diversity of functioning is noted when the content is distinguished from the act of knowing. Although foundational theology recognizes the importance of epistemological inquiry into the content of knowing, its primary concern is with ontological inquiry into the act of knowing. In fact, epistemology can be subsumed under ontology precisely because the structures of being in the world have both a formal and dynamic character. Foundational theology is a transcendental analysis of the activity involved in theological reflection. It responds to the question: How is theology part of our being in the world?

The self is the starting point for the development of foundational theology. Decisions must be made about the intelligibility of experience and the credibility of our reflections. When we talk about experience we must be very careful not to assign meanings to this concept which belong to developed epistemologies instead of turning to the primary manifestations of our subjectivity. Explanatory models emerge out of our subjectivity. It is the experience of self that enfranchises epistemological paradigms with meaning and not epistemology that defines the experience of ourselves. Sometimes the resonances which are sounded between the immediate experience of ourselves and a philosophical paradigm make the philosophical position appear so credible that the primacy of the self in the determination of meaning is blurred.

Even though the concept of selfhood may reach far beyond the boundaries of conscious experience, it is only by paying close attention to the data of consciousness that we can understand why a definition of personal identity is acceptable to us. A methodology is fruitful when through the educated use of the imagination it provides images which illuminate contours of reality recognizable within the boundaries of self experience. Even the most rigorous methodological models within scientific disciplines appeal, implicitly if not explicitly, to the immediate experience of self for justification. Otherwise, the world which they explore lies only in the realm of possible worlds but it is not experienced as part of the real world.

Theology is foundational only when it is talking about the real world of experience. Or, we may say, theology is foundational only when it illuminates the foundations of *our* being in the world. Subjectivity is the center of foundational theology. Not only do we begin with the experiencing subject, but the immediate experience of subjectivity remains the criterion for intelligibility and credibility.

The search for a method adequate for the development of a foundational theology is a major issue. The structures of being which we seek to understand are intimately intertwined with the being that we are. Thus the structures of being which we seek to understand are ready at hand. They must be illumined. There is no a priori justification for the assumption that this is a task more suitable for the scientist than for the poet. There is nothing clear and distinct about the foundations of our being in the world. As was noted by Alfred North Whitehead, those elements which are necessary for experience and constitute its possibility are invariably present to experience. They are not boldly marked by contrasting appearances and therefore lie dimly and vaguely in the background of thought.[6] The characteristics and meanings of these foundational structures must be elicited from the depths of experience so that they have some surface manifestations. The only way we can judge whether a method elicits structures from experience instead of imposing structures on experience is by focusing the method on the experience of self consciousness as our reality principle. Although we can be deceived by our own self knowledge, the immediacy of consciousness is our primary experience and it is only available through the reflections of consciousness on consciousness. Foundational theology grapples with the notion of a reality principle because this principle invests other claims with meaning.

The avoidance of this fundamental task was possible only when there was general tacit acceptance of a single notion of intelligibility. The paradigms of meaning which dominated and unified broad cultural movements no longer claim widespread acceptance. Theology turns toward foundational questions because no single model of intelligibility or principle of reality informs speculations in dogmatic theology. Before we can say yes or no to a system of reflection, we must decide what we mean by the assent to what is real in our experience.

There is neither an Archimedian point from which we can objectively observe the primary experience of self, nor is there a primitive consciousness unencumbered with meaning internal to the experience of the self which avails itself as a radical point of departure for foundational theology. The immediacy of consciousness is not a phenomenological counterpart to Locke's *tabula rasa*. When Henri Bergson referred to intuition as immediate consciousness he was very much aware that consciousness is first experienced through its embodiment and connectedness with the world. He referred to immediate consciousness as a knowledge "which is contact and even coincidence."[7] The separation between the objects of consciousness and *pure* consciousness is an illusion and an example of what Whitehead called the fallacy of misplaced concreteness.

Whatever we mean by *reality* involves the process of experiencing the world. Not only is there a primacy to the *concept* of the *act* of knowing in foundational theology but there is, in fact, a primacy to the *act* of knowing. Our concepts are transcended by the fullness of action and this action is imbedded in the world. The richness of this action is the ground of our appeal for meaning and reality. The tension of inquiry emerges out of the inadequacies of specific thought contents as an expression of thought action. The dialectic between the content and act of knowing promotes the movement of thought.[8] Thus, a method determines the characteristics of a process of experiencing. The feeling of reality is marked by the release of tension associated with glimpses of the unity between the content and act of knowing. This feeling enfranchises a method. We then trust a method to make pronouncements on the shape and meaning of objective experience.

A method which appeals to the immediacy of consciousness is not seeking simplicity but begins in the middle of our experience of the world. This experience belongs to the fullness of our historical situation. We begin amidst a developed language and culture.

Beginning with immediate experience places us in the middle of life and in the middle of the world. This insight into method concurs with Paul Ricoeur's suggestion that "The beginning is not what one finds first; the point of departure must be reached, it must be won."[9] The point of departure, a radical beginning for foundational theology, is an ontological notion and not a temporal notation. Foundational theology moves toward its roots in being. Thus, the origins of foundational theology are disclosed through its own workings. The beginnings of foundational theology are actually a dialectical achievement.

III

There remains the practical problem of entering into the search for a point of departure. Even when we recognize that the proper origins for foundational theology are ontological in character, we must begin with surface manifestations of our concrete existence. Consciousness of consciousness manifests a double intentionality. It intends itself and it intends the world. The disparity between the fullness of self present to the act of inquiry and the poverty of conceptualization involving self and world initiates a movement toward a unified horizon. The envisagement of this horizon gives foundational theology a practical point of departure.

The dialectical relationship between the act and content of knowing continually calls into question our conceptualization of the world. The questions that we pose to our conceptualization of the world extend the boundaries of the world beyond the achievements of the sciences. We cannot investigate the horizon of our being in the world through the contents of scientific achievements precisely because the horizon includes the world determined by the range of questions which transcend the contents of the known.

The horizon of our experience is defined in terms of the range of questions available to the inquirer. Questioning the act of questioning gives us solid footing for illuminating the horizon under which foundational theology will proceed. As Emerich Coreth notes in *Metaphysics*, the act of questioning is undeniable. It is impossible to call into question the possibility of questioning without implicit contradiction.[10] The act of questioning can be unconditionally posited in the middle of experience. Thus, the act of questioning defines the horizon of experience and offers itself as a practical starting point for foundational theology.

There are no artificial limits that can be imposed on the range of questions available to an inquirer since any assigned limit can itself be called into question. In principle, the only limit to questioning that can be formulated is the complete set of answers to the complete set of questions. This corresponds to Bernard Lonergan's definition of transcendent being. Being is the objective of the pure desire to know. Being is the complete set of answers to the complete set of questions.[11] The unrestricted striving of the intellect defines the horizon of questioning and therefore the definition of the horizon can include nothing less than the full scope of being. Anything less than the complete set of answers to the complete set of questions allows for another question and is not a limiting concept. Of course, this only means that if foundational theology takes as its practical point of departure an intellectual pattern of experience, then "transcendence is the elementary matter of raising further questions."[12] Within the intellectual pattern of experience the horizon can be extended into a limiting concept by focusing on the act of questioning.

The identification of the horizon of questioning with being is simply the recognition of the indiscernability of two identities. "How do things stand in being?" is no less of an inquiry than the search for the complete set of answers to the complete set of questions. Being is a supreme heuristic notion that will correspond to the limiting concepts which emerge out of any pattern of experience. It doesn't really matter where foundational theology defines its practical point of departure. Provisional horizons are fused only in the horizon of being itself. What lies beyond any provisional horizon are questions that have not yet come to bear on a method. We can, however, by understanding the act of questioning, transcend any provisional horizon by raising the simple question of its finality. Only the horizon of being remains as a limit to the question of limits. The dialectical movement of thought continually extends boundaries of inquiry so that a discipline such as foundational theology must proceed under the horizon of being. This does not mean that foundational theology takes being as the object of inquiry. Being is the horizon of foundational thinking as defined by questioning. The envisagement of being as the horizon under which foundational theology will develop determines the meaning of primary notions such as *reality* and *intelligibility*. Thus, even the signification of the word *meaning* is rooted in the ontological question, "How do things stand in being?"

The importance of recognizing being as the horizon of foundational theology is primarily methodological. Foundational theology cannot fully develop under provisional horizons. Being is the supreme heuristic notion. This protects foundational theology from reductionistic methods. David Tracy has noted that "What lies beyond my horizon consists not principally of answers but rather of *questions* that are meaningless and insignificant."[13] The envisagement of being as a horizon means that foundational theology cannot ignore questions of ontological meanings.

Our insight into the point of departure for foundational theology is regulative and not constitutive. The manifestation of being is the context for meaning and reality. The question, "How do things stand in being?" defines the quest for intelligibility. We have no new content for investigation. We have a question to ask of experience. The question, "How things stand in being," thematizes the range of experiences that properly belong to the subject as subject.

Thus, it is within the range of foundational theology to investigate the ontological significance of the word of God. This is why it can be said that in foundational theology the hermeneutical task is understood to be the disclosure of ontological meanings which give existential importance to the religious uses of language.

IV

Does this mean that foundational theology requires metaphysics? The role of ontology in foundational theology is not clear. The envisagement of being as the horizon of inquiry extends the responsibilities of foundational theology so that ontological questions are rendered meaningful. But, there is no directive on how this ontological vision is to be incorporated into the methods of foundational theology. Being is the horizon of inquiry, and thus it is not an object of inquiry. Being could be an object of inqure only if we accepted a provisional horizon as the horizon of being. Even in this case, the horizon would be transcended before it could be an object for investigation. Being appears in the dialectical movement of thought not as an object but as a goal.

Of course, it is only in the dialectic between the act and content of knowing that the concept of a horizon is meaningful. We can move toward the horizon even though the horizon is not an object of our inquiry. The emphasis in foundational theology is on the structure of the act of knowing. But, the fullness of the act of knowing intends a content. The movement toward the horizon is a dialectical movement involving both act and content. The language of dialectical movement is multifunctional. It facilitates passage into new areas of experience and it concretizes the content of knowing. Thus, language has reference to both the act and content of knowing.

The concern for being is many layered. The language of movement intends a content and the language of content intends a movement. Ontological vision is a concern for movement as much as it is a study of structure. Foundational theology must comprehend both requirements in the examination of the sacrament of the word of God.

The polyvalence of language remains on the deepest levels of consciousness. No quest for simplicity or depth will resolve the ambiguities of language which are bound to the dialectical nature of thinking. Language in the service of thought always has at least two functions. This has profound methodological implications for determining the role of ontology in foundational theology. Adequacy must be adjudicated in relationship to the movement of thinking toward the horizon of being as well as through traditional criteria, coherence, clarity, etc., for the evaluation of content.

The hope that the philosopher or theologian can discover a univocal language as a tool for the investigation and expression of experience is unrealistic. Because thinking has more than one function, there is no single method or language which can systematically unravel the pluralism of experience. Even within the exact sciences when an object is present to experience, complementarity of methods is sought in the investigation of unknown functions. Ontology is complicated by the fact that its object is not an object but a boundary for multiple patterns of experience. There must be more than one point of departure for approaching this horizon. Thus, there is more than one method for the development of an ontological vision within foundational theology.

Metaphysical inquiry can be used by foundational theology when philosophical discourse is understood to be an experience on the way to the horizon of being. It should be recognized that different methods nuance the character of that experience. Thus, metaphysical conceptions of knowing and language are here not intended to provide bedrock for the translation of theology into philosophy. This leads to reductionism and the truncation of experience. The metaphysical journey toward being is intended to intensify our experience of selfhood and reality and thereby expand the context for theological meaning. The philosopher's trade is akin to that of the poet in his service to foundational theology. The philosopher can provide images, or discern symbols and patterns resident within experience which illumine, qualify, and sometimes transform the meaning of reality. The philosopher must have the freedom of the poet to explore new images if he is to adequately serve theology. It is the dialectical relationship between the act and content of knowing that will move the philosopher toward the horizons of experience and give to foundational theology its ontological vision. The first principles of ontology or epistemology are only images within the content of the known which will be transcended in the fullness of the act of knowing. A positivism in the construction of first principles only retards the dialectical achievements of thinking. In its quest for an ontological vision, foundational theology issues a call for a truly speculative metaphysics.

Speculative philosophy reaches toward the horizon of being through a free play of the imagination. The imaginative generalization of immediate experience provides a context for the elementary steps of transcendence which issue out the dialectical corrective of the knowing act. The images of reflective thinking confront the act of knowing with the call for realization. The inadequacies of these images raise questions for the future achievements of thinking. Ontology is language in the state of becoming. The corresponding emergence of images and experiences serves well the need in foundational theology to enrich the reality principle.

Metaphysical inquiry is a preliminary investigation intended to render more acutely the character of experience and to disclose the range of meanings present to experience. There is no finality to the insights of metaphysics. Thinking is a process and the images which emerge out of metaphysical inquiry only lead us toward the horizon of being. Thus, basic metaphysical categories are *heuristic* structures for the movement through experience which deepen our appreciation of reality but never exhaust its possibilities. The ontological significance of metaphysical categories resides not as importantly in the objects of their references as in their participation in the movement of thought toward the horizon of being. The content of metaphysical inquiry, however, is important since it makes demands upon the dialectic between content and act. The content of reflection gives concreteness to the present moment of thinking. The dialectical movement transcends the formulations of metaphysical inquiry but these formulations make the dialectical movement possible. In ontology, the descriptive function of language gives way to movement. This does not annul the descriptive function of language; it merely indicates that the concrete achievements of thought are multifunctional.

Foundational theology can use metaphysical reflections to enter into a neighborhood of thinking which might otherwise be closed to it. Metaphysics informs theology of contours in the landscape of experience which nuance principles of intelligibility and reality. Since this experience of reality will be used implicitly or explicitly in theological judgments, familiarity with the neighborhood gives the theologian more freedom to plan and execute his work.[14] Dogmatic theology remains independent from specific metaphysical formulations but it requires the ontological vision which can accompany metaphysical reflection to enfranchise its own insights with reality and meaning.[15]

The loss of a center of reality in the life of modern man emphasizes the need for an ontological vision in foundational theology. Metaphysical inquiry serves this need by providing images which initiate the movement toward the horizon of being. The intuitive grasp of meaning and reality can be brought into clearer relief by metaphysical speculation. This vision will grow in importance as foundational theology enters into its complementary task of locating the religious uses of language in lived experience. Metaphysical speculation can contribute to the sensitivity needed for the more concrete task of determining and interpreting transcendent functions present in the gamut of life.

Conceptions of dialectical throught processes give structural significance to transcendence but the real need in religious life is to locate corresponding concrete manifestations of transcendence. Acts of knowing intend a content for completion; and transcendence in the dialectical movements of knowing requires a content for a beginning. The ontological vision comes to fruition in the analysis of concrete achievements. The phenomenological interpretation of lived experience is the second phase in the development of foundational theology.

Transcendence is a dialectical act in reference to a specific content. The subjectivity that is expanded in the analysis of the questioning act to bear witness to transcendence has objective correlates. This is merely an expression of the double intentionality of reflective consciousness. What is important for foundational theology is that these objective correlates can be located in lived experience. Accordingly, the hermeneutical task in foundational theology is to elicit from experience the objective correlates of transcendent acts. This means that foundational theology discloses the characteristic indications of the need for transcendence evidenced in the incompleteness of symbols for thought. These symbols find completion only as transcended in the fullness of the act of knowing.

A phenomenological method enriched by an ontological vision scans the breadth of experience for affirmations of meaning or other

46   THE COMMUNION OF POSSIBILITY

occasions which call into question their own self sufficiency. As Langdon Gilkey suggests, secular understanding fails to provide symbolic forms capable of thematizing the character of secular existence.[16] The incompleteness of secular thought generates an unintelligible residue of fragmentary and transitory experiences. It is the hidden wealth of possible meanings within this residue that foundational theology seeks to unveil.

We can see more clearly the role of an ontological vision. It does not confer validity on phenomenological interpretations of experience, but this vision expands the range of meanings and experiences available to phenomenological inquiry. The ontological vision becomes in itself an experience to be noted. The vision of possibility renders more acutely the vision of actuality.

Recognition of the withdrawal of meaning, the loss of God and the incompleteness of symbols are all occasions for future dialectical achievement. The fragmentary and transitory experiences in secular life find new meanings in transcendent acts. But these are meanings which are in process and have no necessary claim to ultimacy. It is the process that approaches the horizon of being.

Foundational theology is not to be confused with natural theology. On both levels of inquiry, the seeking of an ontological vision and the phenomenological interpretation of lived experience, foundational theology is concerned with the dynamic activity of theological construction and not the express claims of dogmatic theology. The being underway of foundational theology is an apology for the importance and meaningfulness of dogmatic theology. When the notion of word as event becomes a reality, the sacrament of the word of God has a foundational context.

Notes

1. Karl Barth, *Church Dogmatics I:I* (Edinburgh: T. & T. Clark, 1936), p. 15.
2. *Ibid.*, p. 31.
3. Hugh T. Kerr (ed.), *A Compend of Luther's Theology* (Philadelphia: Westminster, 1936), p. 4.
4. *Ibid.*, p. 99.
5. For a brief and informative analysis of various meanings for the word "hermeneutics" see Langdon Gilkey, *Naming the Whirlwind: The Renewal of God-Language* (Indianapolis: Bobbs-Merrill, 1969), pp. 191-192, footnote 2.

6. Alfred North Whitehead, *Modes of Thought* (New York: Macmillan, Free Press Edition 1938), p. vii.
7. Henri Bergson, *The Creative Mind* (New York: Philosophical Library, 1946), p. 32. Also see Chapter IV, "Philosophical Intuition," for Bergson's fascinating account of the development of metaphysical insights.
8. See Emerich Coreth, *Metaphysics*, English edition by Joseph Donceel (New York: Herder and Herder, 1968). The dialectic of concept and act is developed by Maurice Blondel and used by Coreth.
9. Paul Ricoeur, *The Symbolism of Evil* (New York: Harper and Row, 1967), p. 348.
10. Coreth, p. 48.
11. Bernard Lonergan, *Insight: A Study of Human Understanding* (New York: Philosophical Library, Revised Student's Edition, 1958), p. 348, p. 350.
12. *Ibid.,* p. 635.
13. David Tracy, "Horizon Analysis and Eschatology," *Continuum,* Vol. 6, No. 2 (Summer, 1968), p. 169.
14. Heidegger often refers to the neighborhood in which poetry and thinking dwell. I use this image cautiously because I have a different understanding of the possibilities for approaching the horizon of being. I suggest that metaphysical speculations in the dialectical process of thinking contribute to an ontological vision. The polemic against metaphysics fails to recognize the polyvalence of language rooted in the dialectic between the content and act of knowing.
15. An ontological vision is not only the achievement of metaphysical reflection. As Heidegger has indicated, poetry dwells in the neighborhood of being. The theologian may well seek an alliance with the poet instead of the metaphysician. See Nathan Scott, *The Wild Prayer of Longing: Poetry and the Sacred* (New Haven: Yale University Press, 1971) for the development of the suggestion that poetry has an ontological vision.
16. Gilkey, p. 250.

48

CHAPTER IV

A PHILOSOPHICAL
INTERPRETATION
OF HERMENEUTICS

I

ogito ergo sum witnesses to the
fundamental connectedness be-
tween thinking and being. Descartes' attempt to destroy the foundations
of his former opinions could not sever the relationship between thinking
and being. The distinctive character of the relationship between thinking
and being is present even within the confines of radical doubt. The
presence of "I think" and "I am" appear when there is release from the
turmoil of manipulative relationships with the world of experience.

The abstract formulation, I am — I think, is only the skeletal expression for the immediate experience given in the consciousness of consciousness. The affirmation of consciousness is a *corollary* to consciousness of consciousness. The *meaning* of conscious experience is clothed
with our relatedness to the world. Consciousness is not a deeper reality
mediated by the world and thereby hidden by the world. Immediate
experience is of the world and when consciousness appears to consciousness it is always bound to the world. Thus, the expression of the world to
myself is a matter of existential concern. Our imbeddedness in the world
makes questions about the world questions of our own destiny.
Metaphysical questions are also existential questions.

The exterior appearance of metaphysical categories has often given
the philosopher a false sense of objectivity which has led reflection away
from the interior world. In fact, metaphysical categories explore dimensions of subjectivity and their meanings are misunderstood if they are
abstracted from the affirmations of a primal connectedness between
thinking and being. Paul Ricoeur has given significant expression to this
theme when he said: "Cosmos and psyche are two poles of the same
expressivity; I express myself in expressing the world; I explore my own
sacrality in deciphering that of the world."[1]

Metaphysical explorations into the meaning and significance of language are specific attempts to disclose basic characteristics of the expres-

sion of man's subjectivity. Metaphysical categories are heuristic structures used by reflective thinking in its increasing self consciousness.[2] There is a reciprocal relationship between the development of metaphysics and the dialectical growth of understanding. As thought comes of age, metaphysical reflections are necessary to elicit the complex of possibilities which surround the givenness of experience and constitute our openness to the future. However, metaphysics is dependent upon the dialectic between the content and the act of knowing as a fundamental datum for the progressive generation of categories and as a court of actuality for the conferment of existential meaning upon the range of metaphysical speculations. The apparent circularity of metaphysical reflections is not really an important problem if the responsibility of metaphysics is to lead us into new regions of experience and extend the meaning of reality. This is an interior movement and not a search for objective knowledge. What we can see is far more important to metaphysical reflection than what we can prove. The movement of thought is stamped with the excitement of self realization or possible realization when new possibilities are disclosed in their organismic connection with the state of the self. The "sense of reality" is an organic metaphor overladen with the images of seeing, hearing, tasting, smelling and feeling. A sense of reality is not an abstraction. Circularity in reflection is a necessary accompaniment of the fundamental reciprocity between "I think" and "I am." Metaphysical reflection is abstract and devoid of understanding unless it reveals a connectedness with the excitements of organismic existence. A search for proof which is not overladen with a sense of reality is meaningless and search for proof when there is a sense of reality is superfluous. The significance of metaphysical reflection must be decided by what we can see.[3]

Sensual images of organismic connectedness, seeing, hearing, feeling, etc., give definition to the character of experience to which we appeal as we move toward the horizon of being. The primal undifferentiated organismic sense of reality is a dim apprehension of a relatedness marked by conscious affirmations of "I see," "I hear," "I feel," "I taste," or "I smell." The "I think" and the "I am" are bound together so that as the vast range of meanings lurking below the surface of experience are gradually disclosed in the movement of thinking they will have the sensual character of organismic connectedness.

The basic notation for what we mean by *reality* in the development of metaphysical understanding must refer to *our feelings* of connectedness with the world. The focus on feelings as the most concrete element in experience is an acknowledgement of the basic fact of our relatedness but also an appeal for heuristic methodological structures which contribute to the determination of imaginative patterns of meaning within the range of felt patterns of relatedness. Of course, in the dialectical movement of thought the heuristic structures of a method can expand the range of feelings. A sense of reality can exceed its point of departure but it can never cease to be a *sense* of reality. The disconnection of thought from the complexity of organismic existence empties patterns of understanding of their existential meanings. There is a primacy of feelings in our notations of reality which must be secured as the basic principle of explanation. The idea of a thing or object which is felt is an abstraction from the primacy of feeling. Reality finds its meaning in the feeling, the seeing, the hearing, the tasting and the smelling and not in constructs abstracted from immediate experience.

Thus, metaphysical inquiry into the meaning of language seeks definition within the primacy of feeling. Categories must emerge which exhibit the place of language in the organismic patterns of relatedness. A deep sense of the reality of language does not issue from a correspondence between words as abstractions and objects which are abstracted from feeling. The deeper meanings of language are determined by the functioning of language in the organismic complexity of existence. It becomes the responsibility of metaphysical inquiry to imaginatively construct schemata which illuminate and differentiate the gathering of feelings acknowledged as reality. There is no getting behind feeling. Metaphysical analysis seeks to discern patterns of feelings and their functions in the passage of experience.

Since there is no getting behind feelings in the analysis of experience, analysis must examine the patterns or forms of relatedness manifested in the disclosure of feelings. The distinction between matter and form, feelings and patterns or relatedness, is an analytic distinction derived from abstraction. The abstractions of form are punctuated by the actuality of feelings but they cannot comprehend the fullness of a situation. The dialectical movement of thinking in which the act of knowing always transcends the content of knowing is a victory of the concrete over abstract formulations.

The usual distinctions sought between matter and form are in an organismic context more properly viewed as distinctions between actuality and possibility. Feelings and forms of relatedness are not distinguishable in actuality. There is, however, a distinction between that which is felt and that which is not felt. The progressive emergence of feelings, the evolution of experience, and the expansion of reality consciousness all suggest the movement from possibility to the actuality of feelings. Preliminary metaphysical categories must try to account for experience in its becoming. They will initiate the dialectical movement of metaphysics, a journey into new feelings.

II

Elementary categories should correspond to the immediate presentation of experience in self awareness. Thus they do not refer to what are necessarily our simplest or clearest experiences. Instead of beginning with a completed system, we begin with a few tools that are suggested by experience and will eventually be elaborated by the demands of experience. Elementary metaphysical categories should be viewed as the heuristic structures of a radically empirical method. These categories are not to be equated with units of objective reality although they constitute what we mean by our assent to reality.

As already noted, the prime fact in a fundamental description of actuality is the occasion of feeling. Since this is what we mean by reality, the occasion of feeling is the notion to which we return in the exploration of our world. Explanation is completed only when the occasions of feeling which constitute the meaning of an experience have been disclosed to consciousness.

Alfred North Whitehead aids this investigation into the primacy of feelings through his extensive development of a parallel conception to occasions of feeling alternately referred to as actual occasions, epochal occasions, occasions of experience and actual entities in *Science and the Modern World, Religion in the Making, Adventures of Ideas,* and *Process and Reality.*[4]. His descriptions of actual entities correspond to what we mean by the primary experience of reality. As he says in *Process and Reality,* "actual entities are drops of experience" and "the analysis of an actual entity into 'prehensions' (feelings) is that mode of analysis which exhibits the most concrete elements in the nature of actual entities."[5] The analysis of language usage and higher phases of experience will depend upon the development of basic categories such as "actual occasions" in concert with the insights of Whitehead. However, the intent of the investigation continues to be a transcendental inquiry into the possibilities and structure of specific discourse. Therefore, metaphysical insight has primarily methodological significance.[6]

The objectification of Whitehead's categories results from misunderstanding. For example, although actual entities are the final real things which make up the world, Edward Pols has correctly noted that "we cannot give any concrete examples of actual entities."[7] The actual entity should be understood as an explanatory notion derived from immediate experience. The actual entity is a notation for the primal experience of actuality as occasions of feeling.

Just as there is need for notation to speak of the primal experience of actuality there is need for a notation to speak of the primal experience of possibility evidenced in the dialectical movements of thought. The movement of thought presents itself to consciousness as more than feeling. It is also process. That which was not present to consciousness becomes present to consciousness. That which was not an occasion of feeling becomes an occasion of feeling. Possibility is the transcendental ground for change.

Whitehead's notation corresponding to the range of possibilities is the realm of eternal objects, the realm of pure potentials for the specific determination of fact, or the realm of forms of definiteness.[8] Although we may find occasion to use Whitehead's notation, the realm of eternal objects has been an awkward and confusing expression for which we will simply substitute the more natural expressions, the range of possibilities and forms of possibility.

The immediate experience of feelings and process become methodologically formalized as actual occasions and forms of possibility. They are principles of explanation which adjudicate reality in terms of its basic expression as feelings and change. The assignment of reality to understanding is deficient in meaning if explanation is fundamentally disconnected from occasions of feelings and forms of possibility. Metaphysical analysis is the fundamental context for the establishment of meaning. This does not mean that all thinking must have a metaphysical scope. It does mean that the understanding of a discipline requires transcendental metaphysical inquiry. For example, although the creation of the poet need not be metaphysical in character, the significance and meaning of the act of creating is a proper object of transcendental metaphysical inquiry.

The development of metaphysical categories beyond immediate experience is an act of disciplined imagination seeking to disclose the connectedness of these categories with a broad range of human endeavors. A discipline can be rendered meaningful through transcendental inquiry even though the specific content of the discipline remains untouched by the investigation. This is important to remember as we develop the meaning of the conception of possibility.

Forms of possibility are not subject to direct experience. They are manifested in conjunction with the becoming of actual occasions. They are, however, not bound to any specific actual occasion. Whitehead gives a working definition of eternal objects in *Process and Reality* which supports this suggestion. "Any entity whose conceptual recognition does not involve a necessary reference to any definite actual entities of the temporal world is called an 'eternal object.' "[9] Forms of possibility (eternal objects) are a methodological structure used to elicit from experience an elaboration of the primal experience of possibility.

Structures descriptive of actuality and possibility are conjoined to explain what we mean by reality in higher phases of experience. New categories are developed as a result of the exigencies of method and seldom are they directly descriptive of experience. Actual occasions and forms of possibility are the only fundamental descriptive categories which we have sanctioned for transcendental inquiry. They are the conditions of process to which we must always return.

III

Immediate experience is conscious experience. This does not imply that consciousness is the simplest form of relationship. In fact, the notion of the actual entity as an occasion of feelings (relationships) is manifested within consciousness but it is not an explanation of consciousness.

Philosophical inquiry begins amidst the complexities of higher phases of experience. There is a givenness to consciousness. What we mean by reality is grounded in conscious experience but consciousness remains opaque to its own foundation. That is, there is no immediate disclosure of the foundations of consciousness intuited by consciousness. We must work to come to an understanding of higher phases of experience even though our sense of reality is itself derived from higher phases of experience.

The basic unit of reality, occasions of feeling, derived from consciousness does not essentially require consciousness. There is no reason for us to assume that feelings, relationships, are a special property of consciousness. It may be that consciousness is a special property of relationship. It is impossible to talk of consciousness without talking about relationships but it is not impossible to envisage relationships without consciousness. On a psychological level of explanation unconscious relationships have long been considered very important. For example, Charles Brenner says that a fundamental hypothesis in psychoanalytical theory is "the proposition that consciousness is an exceptional rather than a regular attribute of psychic processes."[10]

Actual occasions are explanatory elements. They do not require explanation because they are what we mean by reality. It is consciousness that needs explanation. Using actual occasions as the heuristic structures of a radically empirical method we must try to interpret "the proposition that consciousness is an exceptional rather than a regular attribute of psychic processes." Careful attention must be given to how we experience consciousness. For example, the metaphor, "stream of consciousness," is misleading. Immediate experience is not continuous. Whitehead sometimes refers to actual occasions as epochal occasions. This is a recognition that the basic notation for reality belongs to immediate experience and that an extensive continuum is an abstraction from a multiplicity of immediate experiences.

Immediate experience understood as an occasion of feeling is only confused and distorted if we force it onto an extensive continuum or a stream of consciousness. Consciousness is not itself an entity to be observed. Consciousness of consciousness is a phenomenon to be explained by reference to actual occasions and forms of possibility. The metaphor, "stream of consciousness," would suggest that consciousness is not an exceptional attribute of psychic processes but the foundation of psychic processes. If that were true, consciousness would remain an inexplicable surd in the analysis of higher phases of experience. There would be no basis for the comparative illumination of conscious states with unconscious states. But, it is by no means self evident that consciousness is continuous through psychic processes. We should heed William James' observation, "I am as confident as I am of anything that, in myself, the stream of thinking is only a careless name for what, when scrutinized, reveals itself to consist chiefly of the stream of my breathing."[11] Also, as psychoanalysts have long observed, parapraxes and wit are rooted in the discontinuities of consciousness and the consequent interferences of unconscious processes. What is evident is that although consciousness accompanies our immediate experience of reality, consciousness is not an explanatory principle but itself needs to be explained. Consciousness comes and goes. A theory of consciousness emerges out of the interplay of actual occasions and forms of possibility. Actual occasions and forms of possibility accompany consciousness because they are the possibility for consciousness. Thus, we can say that primal elements are discovered in conscious experience which are not identical with consciousness. This means that the quest for transcendental phenomenology issues in the necessity for transcendental metaphysics. Categories for the explanation of what makes consciousness possible are derived from consciousness but no longer can function within the brackets of an eidetic reduction.

The basic categories, actual occasions and forms of possibility, must describe elementary patterns of relationship. This, however, is confusing. Actuality is described as occasions of feeling but there is no indication of what is felt. The problem is that there is no sanction to talk about feelings in terms other than occasions of feeling and forms of possibility. We have no other categories for what is concrete in our experience.

This appears to be a circular and somewhat awkward use of language. On closer inspection it is clear that we are in fact only remaining true to our commitment to experience. If reality is experienced as occasions of feeling and forms of possibility, there can be no other reference for what is felt without the arbitrary introduction of new concepts. Feelings or forms of possibility can be the objects of feelings. On the most basic level of description these are the only two possibilities. Of course, combinations of feelings are not excluded from consideration in the organization of complex experience. In every case, simple or complex, feelings are explained in terms of other occasions of feelings and forms of possibility. New structures are introduced into the explanatory scheme in accordance with functional needs, but these new structures are merely the elaboration of basic experimental categories. Whitehead refers to the feelings of occasions of feeling as physical prehensions (feelings) and the feelings of forms of possibility as conceptual prehensions. Neither form of relationship implies consciousness.[11]

Physical and conceptual prehensions are descriptive possibilities derived from the immediacy of experience for the elaboration of understanding. They are heuristic structures which anticipate the intelligibility of the known instead of phenomenological structures. Such heuristic structures are rooted in experience but they are never bound to the particularity of their origin. Basic categories and their more complex derivatives enrich experience and render observation more acute. A too limited interpretation of empirical method can lead to obscurantism.

A simple categorization of physical and conceptual feelings cannot explain consciousness. Physical feelings are relationships in an occasion of feeling to, what we can only call, other occasions of feeling. In the passage of experience unknown relationships become known in consciousness. It appears that consciousness of relationships is a privileged state of feeling and cannot itself explain more basic relationships. This is also true when we talk of conceptual feelings, relationships to forms of possibility. In the passage of experience unknown possibilities become known in consciousness. Conceptual feelings cannot be identified with consciousness. Consciousness of possibilities is a privileged state of feeling.

The speculation that relationships are nonexistent prior to their manifestation in consciousness is a dubious suggestion. The multiplicity of conscious experiences which form the collective mind of the community in which we live transcends the scope of our own experiences in refutation of an individualistic phenomenalism. Its only when we are — I am — willing to adopt the uncompromising position of a solipcism of the present moment that the notion of relationships as nonexistent outside of my consciousness can gain any currency. Not only must I argue against a community of opinion if I opt for such a radical idealism but I must also fortify myself against the violence of my animal experience. George Santayana clearly noted that it is the exigences of animal life that establish realism and not conscious experience.[12] The immediacy of consciousness is the mediation of our primoridal imbeddedness in the world. The primary categories derived from consciousness are heuristic structures used for the exploration of our basic connectedness with the world. They must in turn constitute the elaborative structures through which we can explain consciousness as a privileged state of feeling.

The key to revealing the structures behind consciousness is the necessity of contrast for consciousness. For example, in the simplest consciousness of color or form there is a need for contrast. To see a circle on a white screen the circle must of a contrasting color. In fact we often talk of a figure *against* a ground. The use of *against* implies a contrast. For an experience to be clear and distinct there must be variability and contrast. In order to ascertain the reliability of my witness to an event I may be asked to distinguish this event from other similiar events. Whether I was clearly conscious of what I experience is decided by my ability to contrast my experience with similar experiences. Ordinary discourse readily connects consciousness with contrasting feelings. Clear thinking, consciousness, awareness, means the ability to discriminate the boundaries of contrast.

Physical and conceptual feelings come into consciousness only when they are united in contrast. A structure is necessary to account for the unified feeling of contrasting feelings. It is not enough that there are a diversity of feelings. The figure must be connected to the ground if it is to be seen. That is, diverse feelings must be united if they are to be contrasting feelings.

In conscious experience it is one function of propositions to draw connections and explicate relationships. Is there an analogue to propositions which lies behind consciousness and stands as its possibility? Can we talk of transcendental propositions which make conscious experience possible? We can and must talk of transcendental propositions if our inquiry is to continue, but we should remember that we are talking of methodological heuristic structures and not physical entities.

The basic propositional structure does not imply consciousness. Transcendental propositions only provide the structural possibility for consciousness. In accordance with Whitehead's *Process and Reality*, I am defining a proposition as an impure potential for the specific determination of matters of fact.[13] A transcendental proposition is a hybrid structure uniting physical and conceptual feelings. The subject of a transcendental proposition is a physical feeling and the predicate of a transcendental proposition is a conceptual feeling. This structurally conjoins actuality with possibility. The simplest proposition would be that in which the predicated forms of possibility are in fact exhibited in the occasion of feelings which constitutes the subject. The feeling of this proposition would involve no contrast and would not flicker into consciousness. More complex propositions may involve a contrast between the predicated forms of possibility and the actuality of the subject. If a relevant contrast is formed, these propositional feelings are conscious feelings.

Propositions are a procedure of an imaginative faculty which lies behind consciousness and makes it possible. I have no intent to reify this transcendental imagination. It serves as an explanatory principle for the experience of consciousness. It illuminates the passage of higher phases of experience. Conscious experience is rooted in the integration of actuality and possibility. The propositional feeling is only a methodological notation for the reality of this integration. To envision the need for such an integration of actuality and possibility below the level of consciousness as the possibility of consciousness bears upon the interpretation of value and meaning on the conscious level of experience. Before occasions of feeling can come into consciousness they must stand in contrast with other possibilities for the integration of feelings. The proposition can in this way lure us toward the actualization of new possibilities. The major function of the proposition is to facilitate passage into new occasions of feeling and these occasions of feeling are what we mean by reality. Thus, the proposition facilitates passage into a larger reality. Consciousness is an accompaniment to the basic passage from one occasion of feeling into another. The interpretation of conscious experience must not be disjoined from the ontological significance of the propositional structure which facilitates the evolution of reality as well as the appearance of consciousness. What appears in consciousness marks the passage of realities below the threshold of awareness. The interpretation of conscious experience must remain aware of important ontological correlates which accompany consciousness but do not themselves come into explicit consciousness. In particular, we must be aware of the ontological analogue to language usage.

Consciousness participates in its own foundation in the use of language. The imaginative roots for consciousness lie in complexes of propositions which conjoin actuality with forms of possibility. However, the propositional structure belongs to consciousness as well as behind consciousness. Through the elaboration of language, consciousness augments the complexity of its own foundation. It is very clear that the range of conscious experience can be expanded through language usage. The disclosure of possibilities within consciousness draws consciousness into new experiences. What is not clear is the importance of conscious disclosures to movements which lie below the experience of consciousness. Consciousness is only a privileged state of relatedness with the world. The isomorphism between language and the transcendental imagination makes language a functional part of our ontological passage through life. The importance of language cannot be evaluated solely on the surface of conscious experience. The propositional disclosure of possibilities lures occasions of feeling into new realizations, but there must be sufficient contrast in propositional feelings for these feelings to be conscious. Conscious propositions may reveal possibilities which are incorporated into transcendental propositions which contribute to the passage of experience but which do not elicit sufficient contrast with existing occasions of feeling to come into consciousness.

Language usage has an ontological significance which is structurally manifested in the propositional structure of becoming. That is, structural considerations indicate that language usage is ontologically significant even though the actualizations of possibilities facilitated by language are sometimes below the threshold of consciousness. This means that there is an ontological dimension to language usage which must be incorporated into models for the interpretation of language. Metaphysical analysis only provides a transcendental notation for the ontological significance of language. The much more difficult task of evaluating the significance of this ontological dimension of language in the interpretation of particular texts and linguistic experiences is not within the range of transcendental analysis. An understanding of meaning through meaning is the function of hermeneutics, but hermeneutical disciplines must be cognizant of the ontological significance of language if they are to illuminate the full range of meanings associated with the many uses of language.

IV

The fundamental connectedness between thinking and being manifested in the presence of consciousness to consciousness and elaborated by metaphysical inquiry into the ontological significance of language suggests a reformulation of the hermeneutical task. A topographic description of language usage would necessarily be multidimensional and correspond with the diverse functions of linguistic structures. The complex synthesis of content and act in understanding the world binds together the many functions of language in single expressions of language. These multifunctional expressions give rise to levels of interpretation and designate the hermeneutical field. Metaphysics is allied with hermeneutics because interpretation is deficient in meaning if it is disconnected from our two elementary tools, forms of possibility and occasions of feeling.

The existence of levels of interpretation compounds the responsibility of interpretation. Points of connection or passages between levels must be uncovered as part of the hermeneutic task. Diverse levels of meaning corresponding to different language functions must be related to each other as interpretation seeks completeness.

Interpretation should, however, not be confused with the simple translation of language from one level of usage to another. The diversity of language functions corresponding to the distinctions between the act and content of knowing constitute only part of the significance of multivocal expression. The image of the depth of language is itself a multivocal expression.

We have recognized that language has at least two different functions. Language points and language carries. That is, language functions ostensively and language functions ontologically. In both functions there is an elaboration of the experience of reality. In fact, the separation of language functions is an analytic distinction and it is not met with in our concrete experience. The importance of making any distinction between the ontological and ostensive functioning of language is to clarify the necessary complexity of hermeneutics. All linguistic expressions are subject to the necessary ambiguity of having functional significance on at least two different levels. Even trivial expressions contribute to the pattern of our being in the world. Recognition of the ontological function of language accentuates the significance of Heidegger's insight that "it is in words and language that things first come into being and are. For this reason the misuse of language in idol talk, in slogans and phrases, destroys our authentic relation to things."[14] Thus, one meaning of the depth of language is that linguistic expressions have ontological importance. The linguisticality of existence — the ontological significance of the propositional structure — suggests that we must have a hermeneutics which is allied with metaphysics.

But, this is not the only important distinction that gives rise to the hermeneutical task. If we were to ignore the ontological functions of language structures we could still detect the presence and importance of multiple meaning expressions. The presence of symbolic as well as direct discourse in mythology, poetry and dreams has been amply documented by studies in the history of religions, literary criticism and psychoanalytic theory. The complications of translation and exegesis in biblical studies have long suggested that the opacity of some expressions, the irreducibility to univocal propositions, is not a failure of language but a wisdom of language. Aside from the negative or positive value assigned to multivalent expressions, they raise the problem of interpretation. To understand a text we must decide what to do with multiple meaning expressions. There is a need for hermeneutics even without any metaphysical insight into the diverse functions of language. There is an ontological depth to language and there is also a depth to language manifested in the capacity of symbols to unify and express a multiplicity of meanings.

Interpretation is a responsibility of philosophical inquiry with or without metaphysics. The same issues and polarities manifest themselves in defining the meaning and responsibility of hermeneutics when investigating descriptive or ontological language functions. This suggests the correspondence that must be part of serious language study.

There are two interpretations of interpretation within the confines of descriptive language functions. Multiple meaning expressions invite expansion or reduction. These are the polarities within which interpretation must define its responsibility. Reductive interpretation of multivalent expressions, symbols, seeks a language of univocal expression. This may be formalized in the hope of creating an ideal language in which ambiguities are sacrificed to logical precision, or first principles may be formulated for the clear expression of the vagaries of human experience, or interpretive models of explanation are sometimes substituted for the text of human experience. In all of these examples the attempt is to remove the ambiguities of multivocal expression by the substitution of language of univocal expression. The commitment to clear and distinct understanding supersedes the possibility that the given ambiguity of symbolic expression may be an essential and deeply significant characteristic of language.

According to the reductive pole of interpretation, hermeneutics should be the destruction of illusion and the dissolution of ambiguity. In this case interpretation is identified with clarification. The important issues surround questions about what is "really" being said, felt, or desired. Symbolic language is to be unmasked so that the authentic situation is visible.

It is this concern with confronting an authentic voice that defines the concerns of the expansive pole of interpretation. It is precisely this concern which gives unity to the two interpretations of interpretation within the confines of descriptive language functions. An expansive hermeneutics begins with the multivocal character of symbolism and seeks to restore to this expression its many variations of meaning. Here, interpretation is seen as a recollection of meaning or an elaboration of meaning in meaning. The expansive conception of interpretation affirms that one of the important functions of multivalent symbols is their capacity for conjoining diverse and sometimes even paradoxical themes. This unity is lost when symbols are translated into a language of univocal expression. At best we would then have unity through the attachment of one proposition to another proposition. The notion of an expansive interpretive framework is a commitment to the integrity of language. The symbol confronts us as an occasion for the expansion of experience. The unity resident within the symbol is the possibility for the elaboration of feeling.

We need interpretation which respects the multivalence of symbols. How can we become hearers of the word? The same problems confront us when we try to construct a hermeneutics with metaphysics. If the act of knowing is separated from the content of the known, we may then be tempted to reductively interpret a living text through its translation into metaphysical categories. The unique relationship of language and world under superficial examination appear to support this interpretation of interpretation. This is just one variation of reductive interpretation. The complexity of symbolic content is ignored because only the ontological dimension of depth can be plumbed in metaphysical analysis. However, the categories in metaphysical analysis have a transcendental foundation and thus have only the status of heuristic structures used for the exploration of the possibilities of experience. Metaphysical categories are structural considerations which are regulative of experience but they are not constitutive of experience. Thus, metaphysical categories can regulatively contribute to the definition of the hermeneutical task, but they cannot actually be substituted for interpretation. Metaphysical insights make demands upon the scope of an interpretive framework. The complicity of language and being render conditional horizons for interpretive thinking inadequate.[15] Metaphysics determines the horizon under which hermeneutical reflection develops, but metaphysics must not pose in the guise of hermeneutical reflection.

A philosophical hermeneutic understands that we must listen carefully to the voice of being as it belongs to language. We must now understand the conjunction of two insights. (1) On the immediate level of conscious experience we defined one pole of the hermeneutical task as an elaboration of meaning in meaning. It is the unique function of symbolic language to give rise to expanded experience. And (2) from metaphysical inquiry it was clear to us that it is the function of the propositional structure to facilitate the passage through experience and the emergence of new realities. Thus, thinking and being are intimately related in the functions of language. The elaborative definition of the hermeneutical task on the immediate level of consciousness is now expanded to incorporate the regulative insights of metaphysical inquiry. Metaphysics serves hermeneutics but it is not hermeneutics.

Transcendental metaphysical reflection indicates to hermeneutics that an elaboration of meaning in meaning, the recollection of meaning facilitated by the many voices of language, is inextricably bound to a recollection of being.

New and important questions are raised by metaphysical reflections on hermeneutics. How do we allow a recollection of meaning to coincide with a recollection of being? How do we allow conscious meanings to announce ontological meanings? How can we see or hear the ontological meanings which dwell in conscious meanings?

Metaphysical findings suggest the significance of these questions. Thus, the future definition of the hermeneutical task includes an elaboration of metaphysical insights and a response to the questions posed by these insights. The metaphysical interpretation of interpretation is a transcendental contribution to the future of hermeneutics.

NOTES

1. Paul Ricoeur, *The Symbolism of Evil* (New York: Harper and Row, 1967), p. 13.
2. This does not preclude the objective significance of metaphysical inquiry. We recognize that metaphysics is basically an imaginative movement within fundamental ontology.
3. Cf. Alfred North Whitehead, *Modes of Thought* (New York: Macmillan Free Press, 1968), pp. 48-49.
4. Alfred North Whitehead, *Science and the Modern World* (New York: Mentor Book, New American Library, 1925); *Religion in the Making* (Cleveland: Meridian Books, World Publishing Co., 1964); *Adventures of Ideas* (New York: Mentor Books, New American Library, 1933); *Process and Reality* (New York: Macmillan Free Press, 1969).
5. Whitehead, *Process and Reality,* p. 23; parenthetical insert is my addition. Whitehead's definition of prehensions as concrete facts of relatedness include two species — positive and negative prehensions. Only positive prehensions can correctly be referred to as feelings.
6. *Ibid.,* p. 11.
7. Edward Pols, *Whitehead's Metaphysics* (Carbondale, Ill.: Southern Illinois University Press, 1963), p. 6.
8. Whitehead, *Process and Reality,* p. 26.
9. *Ibid.,* p. 58.
10. Charles Brenner, *An Elementary Textbook of Psychoanalysis* (Garden City, New York: Doubleday Anchor Books, 1957), p. 2.
11. Whitehead, *Process and Reality,* p. 28.
12. See George Santayana, *Scepticism and Animal Faith* (New York: Dover Publications Inc., 1955).
13. Whitehead, *Process and Reality,* p. 26.
14. Martin Heidegger, *Introduction to Metaphysics* (Garden City, New York: Doubleday Anchor Books, 1961), p. 11.
15. Cf. Emerich Coreth, "From Hermeneutics to Metaphysics," *International Philosophical Quarterly,* Vol. XI, No. 2 (June, 1971), p. 259. "Hermeneutics transcends itself into metaphysics insofar as the openness to being is the transcendental ground of all understanding of the world, of history, and language." I think that Coreth's statement should be viewed as a requirement which expands the hermeneutical task but it should not be viewed as describing the content of hermeneutical reflection.

CHAPTER V

SACRED MARKINGS:
AN ELEMENTARY
TOPOGRAPHY

I

he interpretation of experience can no longer remain exclusively on the plane of conscious happenings. The metaphysical analysis of language suggests that there are two levels of happenings and that conscious experience is a privileged occurrence that marks a more elementary process. The theologian seeking an adequate assessment of the human situation must learn to recognize how conscious meanings announce ontological meanings. A meaningful interpretation of experience cannot be extraneous to experience but should first of all be an illumination of the complex of happenings that constitute experience. The first and most general significance for the meaning of transcendence must be connected to the interpretation of secular experience if the specialized manifestations of the sacred in the world's religions are to have meanings that extend beyond their specificity. Foundational theology moves from its first responsibility of determining the structural possibilities for theological discourse to a second phase of inquiry which locates the sacred markings in conscious experience corresponding to elementary moments of transcendence in the fullness of life.

The mature religious personality discerns sacred markings in the contours of everyday secular life. The interpretation of universal human themes such as birth, puberty, love, marriage, death, boredom, meaninglessness, hope, and vision move man to the frontiers of understanding and even the unsophisticated thinker draws upon images of depth and transcendence to render these experiences intelligible. Foundational theology must survey the landscape of secular experience to determine where the sacred manifests itself. The structural analysis of elementary moments of transcendence quickens our vision of the presence of the sacred in secular life through regulatory demands placed upon the interpretation of any passage through life. The dialectical processes belonging to the passage through life which become obvious in moments of crisis are, after the insights of our transcendental investigation, also discernible in the rhythm of everyday happenings.

Foundational theology complements and extends its elementary structural analysis of transcendence into recognizable regions of concrete experience by the construction of a topographical model using insights from the history of religions, literary criticism and the social sciences. A topographical model of sacred markings is a preliminary consideration in the construction of a doctrine of the church. It indicates the areas of meaning and experience to which the concept of church is significantly connected and thereby provides groundwork for the evaluation of the importance of the church as an institution and as a communion of possibility.

The search for sacred markings is a retrieval of a consciousness of transcendence that can be rooted in forms of secular life. Religion and concern with manifestations of the sacred are bound to the experience of persons having visions, dreaming dreams, sharing hopes, celebrating meanings, feeling feelings that go beyond themselves.[1] These experiences are available and make sense to secular man. In an intellectual pattern of experience Bernard Lonergan says that "transcendence is the elementary matter of raising further questions."[2] We can say that ciphers of transcendence correspond with the vague sense of possibility that accompanies visions, hopes and dreams on the frontiers of experience. A topographical determination of sacred markings is basically an elementary interpretation of the ontological conception of transcendence through translation into moments of transcendence present in regions of concrete experience.

In our concrete experience transcendence is characterized by the presence of an otherness beyond the immediacies of our situation. This otherness may refer to felt realities that primarily rest outside of the boundaries of our situation or the felt need for patterns of meaning that are not enclosed by the boundaries of our situation. The religious valuation given to transcendence depends on several variables such as the enormity of the dimensions of "otherness" present in the experience, the intensity of the feelings, expectations of intelligibility, the worldview of the community and the psychology of the individual. Certainly not all elementary experiences of transcendence receive a religious valuation. Developed conceptions of transcendence and revelation must be able to illuminate the broad range of feelings and experiences that can properly be referred to as sacred markings. The manifestation of the "wholly other" in fear and trembling and John Wesley's Aldersgate Street experience in which he felt his heart strangely warmed are both sacred markings. And, if transcendence is an elementary matter of raising further questions, the discontinuities and unanswered questions present in the secular examination of everyday life are also sacred markings.[3] The emptiness of secular understanding may be positively characterized as the felt need for patterns of meaning not enclosed by the boundaries of secular criteria for the determination of intelligibility. There is no single definition or characterization of sacred markings present in everyday experience. Sacred markings correspond with an elementary definition of transcendence and not with abstract definitions of religion. Transcendence and religion are so intimately intertwined that when we speak of transcendence we are developing a conception of religious man. Mature religious life may be described as a state "being grasped by an ultimate concern," but there are latent religious meanings within the human experience which are lost to foundational theology if we only examine the mature personality. Although we may finally agree with J. Kitagawa that "a religion is thus understood as the particular expression of a universal mode of human reaction to Ultimate Reality," or with Mircea Eliade that "all authentic religious experience implies a desperate effort to disclose the foundations of things, the ultimate reality," our beginning definition of religion is simply the human response to moments of transcendence, sacred markings, in the broad range of experiences.[4] An ultimate concern can be shaped by the growing discernment of the meaning of sacred markings in the maturing personality.

Transcendental reflection has opened the search for sacred markings by showing that the structural meaning of transcendence is the functional connection of actuality and possibility in the ontological passage into new occasions of feeling. Forms of possibility are an "otherness" which surround realizations of actual feeling and condition the passage of actual feelings into future realizations. Forms of possibility define a region of reality which functions as both the ground and goal of actuality. Specific forms of possibility have ingressed into actual occasions of feeling and have thus made determinate the boundaries of these moments of actuality. The realm of possibilities is not coextensive with the boundaries of particular actual occasions but transcends the moment and opens the future to new processes. The elementary meaning of transcendence is the conjunction of actuality and possibility.

The propositional structure is the possibility for the integration of actuality and forms of possibility. In this sense, the propositional form is the structural meaning of transcendence. Elementary acts of transcendence are part of even the simplest expressions of passage that occur below the threshold of consciousness. The ontological structural definition of transcendence tells us that we are looking for what is already at hand. Transcendence is even a part of happenings that are not yet conscious.

The structural understanding of consciousness which always involves the conjunction of possibility and actuality furthers the recognition of the importance of transcendence in everyday life. Consciousness as a privileged happening is itself a marking of transcendence. Consciousness occurs when there is sufficient contrast between what is and what can be — actual feelings and forms of possibility. However, when sharp contrasts occur, it is not consciousness which is observed as a transcendent happening,but it is the object of consciousness that dominates the experience. When a black object is the figure on a white ground, it is not the contrast between figure and ground that grasps our attention but the figure itself.

It is only in reflection that consciousness appears as a transcendent act. We do not notice the possible except in reflection. When the possible appears as the possible instead of as ground for the figure of objective consciousness, experience recognizes that which is other than itself and that which is the judgment on itself. The same uncanny feeling that accompanies the simple psychological examples given by gestalt psychologists to demonstrate the relativity and ambivalence of figure against ground accompanies our sense of reality when the possible appears as "other" along side of the actual. Although all acts of consciousness are acts of transcendence according to the ontological structural definition, it is only when the possible manifests itself as "other" that we can talk about a sacred marking as appearing within the range of conscious experience. Thus, a topographical model does not locate transcendent acts but differentiates among transcendent acts according to various intensities of awareness. What is brought into clear relief by reflection are those areas of relativity, ambiguity and ambivalence in life where the otherness of possibility impinges upon a monolithic secular world in which actuality is too easily identified with reality. A dialectic between the secular world and a world that includes the otherness of possibility, a sacred world, is initiated. We recognize that a concern with the world that focuses on both the ground and telos of creative passage can become ultimately serious. We must begin, however, by gleaning those sacred markings that appear in spite of the secular world's predominant but not ultimate concern with objectivity.

To be of service to the church, theology must be heard. Thus, contemporary theology lays its own foundations in the midst of immediate experience through transcendental reflection and then seeks to determine the implications of these insights in the midst of a secular consciousness of experience. This means that the theologian must understand the language of the secular world and learn to creatively speak to a world which thinks in secular terms.[5] Transcendental reflection in foundational theology fortifies the vocational identity of the theologian but it does not speak in a language that can ordinarily be heard in the secular marketplace of ideas. In spite of the demonstrated foundational significance of transcendent acts, the meaning of transcendence remains obscure in the secular understanding of everyday life. The concept of transcendence is ontologically significant but has not yet become existentially important. That is, the ontological meaning of transcendence has not been sufficiently interpreted in regions of concrete experience. There has been inadequate representation of transcendent acts in the conscious understanding of experience. The intentionality of conscious acts has led to an objectivity which has obscured the dialectic of actuality and possibility at the roots of consciousness. Sacred markings are everywhere. Foundational theology appeals to the notion of a topographical model because it understands its second task as bringing into clear relief the complicity of transcendent acts in secular life.

II

A topographical model proves nothing. It is merely a map or guide into those regions of experience or self understanding where transcendent acts are less shadowed by prevalent forms of secular understanding. Transcendental reflection has rendered observation more acute and thereby aids the perusal of a plurality of experiences. There is no attempt at a deduction from metaphysical principles; but metaphysical structures are relevant because they anticipate the meaning of intelligibility. Again, we can say that they render observation more acute. They suggest the need for an empirical method that sees experience when it is sober or intoxicated. A topographical model is a tool. It basically is only an image and should be judged by its usefulness in the gathering and evaluation of experience. Adequacy is a more important concept than validity in this search for sacred markings.

We should not proceed with a naive view of secular culture in viewing the dialectic between the sacred and the profane. The diverse theological movements which have fluctuated between celebrations of the secular city and despair over the force of secularization appear to have taken ideology more seriously than experience. As Peter Berger has noted in *A Rumor of Angels*, "there is scattered evidence that secularization may not be as all-embracing as some have thought." There are subterranean rumblings of supernaturalism which coexist with academic rationalism in our culture.[6] The existence of counter-communities of cognitive deviance which highly value supernatural occurrences or beliefs suggests that secularization has not completely erased the sacred markings on the surface of our cultural experience. These enclaves of supernaturalism seek to protect and nourish aspects of self-awareness that can be lost in the residue of rationalism. Even aberrant strivings for an "otherness" which can be viewed as the ground and telos of existence question the permanence of the boundaries fixed by singular concern with objective experience. I do not suggest that theologians need to analyze the broad range of sectarian religious communities or the flourishing astrological subculture to do their own work. The existence of these communities, however, should indicate to him that human experience is not understood as one dimensional even in our modern secularized world. Dimensions of depth can be lost by hasty generalizations about secularization just as dimensions of depth can be lost by hasty generalizations about religion. It is in the pluralism of experience and the accompanying multivalence of symbols that sacred markings manifest themselves.

Transcendental reflection indicates that all passage through life is dependent upon transcendent acts. The theological problem is no longer whether there is or is not a transcendent dimension in human experience. That has been determined by the metaphysical expansion of transcendental reflection. The problem is how and where does this dimension of meaning present itself to self understanding. This is not an attempt to rescue religion from secularism but an attempt to rescue experience from obscurity.

Important regions of experience are often pushed aside because they are not clean well lighted places. Language is not confined to one meaning in these places. Some conscious situations mirror the ambiguity and ambivalence of meanings that are resident in the dialectic of actuality and possibility on the level of ontological passage. It is possible for any experience to mirror its ontological foundations in mature understanding, but there is in every epoch some experiences which are more easily deciphered. These experiences clearly bear witness to their complicity with transcendence.

There are at least seven regions of experiencing which are marked by an ambiguity of levels of meaning because they express characteristics of their ontological foundation in their concrete realization. Of course it would be presumptuous to suggest that there are only seven such regions of expressivity when any realization has roots in transcendent acts. In our experience these seven areas, because they are important, raise questions about the architecture of experience and sometimes appear anomalous in secularized models of self understanding. Paul Ricoeur refers to three of these areas, the cosmic, oneiric, and poetic, as zones of the emergence of symbolism.[7] To these regions we may want to add the comic, ludic, neurotic, and dramatic.[8] The distinctions between regions can never be clearly established. That is not the function of observing them. They all require a complex view of self determination that recognizes the meaning of transcendence. They are part of a topographic interpretation of transcendence but do not exhaust the possibilities for mapping regions of symbolic meanings.

We will review some of the elementary characteristics of these regions for the expression of transcendent acts to see how they influence our understanding of personal experience. Peter Berger refers to these dimensions of experience as signals of transcendence. They are sacred markings in the multiple possibilities for the expressivity of self understanding.

The role of the comic even within a seemingly secular understanding of humanity gives a glimmering of transcendence. Drawing insights from Freud and Bergson and transforming them into his own creative viewpoint, Peter Berger has suggested that the essence of the comic is discrepancy, incongruity and incommensurability.[9] It is basically in the discrepancy between the world of consciousness and the foundational significance of unconscious meanings that we find the essence of the comic. The reason that sex and death play a fundamental role in the comic is that they unmask conscious pretensions about human identity and the dignity of the objective rational view of personhood. Situations are comical when the significance of the possible impinges unexpectedly upon the security of the actual. Ultimately the comic reflects the presence of the human spirit in a world of actual feelings surrounded by a realm of possibilities. As Berger indicates, the comic is a signal of transcendence. It is a sacred marking that becomes intelligible in the recognition of possibility as an ontological qualifier of the present situation. In the comic experience, the realm of possibilities unexpectedly transforms the situation. The comic is a vision of hope because it unveils the presence of possibility which is essentially conjoined with actuality in the passage through existence.

The ludic (play element in experience) dimension of experience and the envisagement of man as *homo ludens* must also be seen as a sacred marking within the range of secular understanding. Play is a stepping beyond the rules of "real" life. It is a temporary suspension of the ordinary world of objectivity.[10] In particular, it is a suspension of time. As with children's play, man ceases to be bound to the exigences of the moment and lives in eternity.[11] Even though Johan Huizinga may have correctly viewed processes of secularization transforming play in professional sports, the televised presentation of professional sports provides a regular and dependable shelter from a passage of time locked in the "serious" business of the world. Play is a sacred marking in the center of life. It points beyond the necessity of clock-time. Time is ruptured; the magic of timeless play is an image of transcendence; play provides a shadowed insight into the contingency of temporal passage.

The poetic dimension of experience is more complex and yet more articulate than comic and ludic manifestations of the sacred. The poetic is also more removed from the rhythm of secular life than the comic and the ludic. The journey into the neighborhood of poetry requires a recovery of sacred sensibilities. The existence of the poetic is a testimony of the sacred to whomever can listen. The poetic experience requires a hermeneutic that goes beyond the scope of this inquiry and thus we will only move to the edge of reflection on poetry and primal thinking.

Poetry is seen as an instrument of communion.[12] This communion is, in its strongest statement, a communion with the gods. It is a penetration into the deepest meanings of transcendence. It becomes a communion of possibility. Heidegger proclaims in *Existence and Being* that "To 'dwell poetically' means: to stand in the presence of gods and to be involved in the proximity of the essence of things."[13] Ricouer quotes Gaston Bachelard as saying that the poetic image "places us at the *origin* of articulate being."[14] Or, from the secularized vision of the Marxist philosopher Ivan Svitak, "Poetry reveals to man the secret aspect of human existence itself, and that has been its function in all myths of the past."[15]

In all of these claims the poem has functions and carries meanings which go beyond, below or behind the surface of human experience. Poetry transcends the immediate givens of objective experience.[16] Poetry is language becoming self conscious of its ontological significance. The poem is an articulate fusion of realms of actuality and realms of possibility. The vocations of philosopher and poet become a shared vocation as both come to mature realization.

Although Heidegger thinks that "The poetic work speaks out of an ambiguous ambiguousness," it is probably the clearest and most distinct sacred marking within the purview of our collective consciousness.[17]

There is very little awareness of the cosmic dimension in secular experience. The mythical and philosophical attempts to penetrate to the ground of being or origin and telos of meaning is conspicuously absent in predominantly secular modes of philosophical analysis. The presence of cosmic dimensions of meaning can only be discerned on the boundaries of secular experience in limiting questions which determine the effective range of positivistic models in the sciences and philosophy. The cosmic dimension of experience is more clearly revealed in the mythology and behavior patterns of premodern or traditional societies than in modern secular society. The historian of religions renews the contemporary quest for cosmic dimensions of ultimacy by unraveling the presystematic ontologies evidenced in the experience of archaic man.[18] The establishment of the real and its identification with the sacred is a function of cosmogonic myths in "traditional," premodern, societies. Thus the demise of metaphysics and the loss of the sacred accompany each other in the making of the modern mind.

It is the historian of religions and not the theologian who can more easily characterize cosmic dimensions of transcendence in the passage of life. Cosmic expressions of transcendence are camouflaged in the modern world. The great religious themes uncovered by the historian of religions in the study of archaic patterns of experience are present in the shadows of the dramatic, oneiric and neurotic dimensions of modern experience. Cosmic dramas influence the life of modern man only as secondary revelations. The histories of supernatural deities revealed to archaic man the meaning and structure of his existential situation. The histories of archaic men now reveal to modern man the meaning and structure of his existential situation. The historian of religions can provide a fund of meanings on which we can draw in the analysis and interpretation of sacred markings in the dramatic context of modern man's secular life.

The sacred markings found in the comic, ludic, poetic, and cosmic dimensions of self understanding give witness to the importance of transcendence as a modifier of persons. In the direct analysis of transcendence and personhood we see the meaning of the power of the sacred manifested positively in the dramatic rendering of destiny and modified by the flexibility of dreams and hopes. Negatively, the fear of the sacred leads to a scotosis of the intellect and a dramatic pattern of life modified by neurotic tensions. Since man's "first work of art is his own living," and "style is in the man before it is in the artistic product," an elementary topography of sacred markings is not complete unless it determines the sacred markings on an architectural model of the psyche.[19]

The dramatic dimensions of experience are marked by transcendence. We must learn to tell our own stories so that we can embody the consciousness of our encounter with transcendence. Sam Keen has even suggested "that telling stories is functionally equivalent to belief in God."[20] The inability to tell stories is an inability to discern the sacred markings in the dramatic dimensions of experience; the loss of a story is a loss of the dramatic component in self understanding. We can't tell our story because we don't know the way about our own experience. The neurotic bias of positivistic methodologies inhibits us from rendering life meaningful in the development of a story.

To recapture the dramatic expressions of transcendence we must reawaken all of the elements of experience that are part of our story. The dispossession of objective consciousness as the primary tool of signification in the dramatic passage through life is first manifested in the recovery of the importance of the body in determining our presence in the world. The body situates us in the world. The body mediates the actuality and presence of others in the world.[21] On the first level of experiencing I agree with Merleau-Ponty that "I am conscious of the world through the medium of my body."[22] Consciousness must go through the body. The body is primary and implicates us in a going-behind consciousness. The unreflected experience of the world through the presence of the body and bodily gesture is a primary region of signification. The pretensions of conscious meaning are humiliated by the priority of bodily significations. The drama that we must portray hints of meanings that transcend consciousness even as we situate ourselves bodily on the stage of living experiences.

The significance of meanings below the threshold of consciousness is posited very strongly by the discovery of the unconscious. The history of dynamic psychiatry is a significant chronicle documenting attempts in the recent past to take seriously a multiplicity of meanings often neglected in objectivist renderings of experience. Psychoanalytic theory and analytic psychology further shatter the illusion that there is only one level of concrete experience.

Psychoanalytic theory goes beyond the simple dispossession of consciousness as the sole arbiter of meaning. One of the fundamental hypotheses in psychoanalysis is that unconscious mental processes constitute the bulk of normal and abnormal mental functioning.[23] Freud says that "mental processes are *essentially* unconscious, and those which are conscious are merely isolated acts and parts of the whole psychic entity."[24]

The textbook proofs for the existence of the unconscious implicate the whole dramatic rendering of sacred markings in unconscious themes. Conscious mental processes cannot adequately account for parapraxes (slips of the tongue, etc.) in everyday experience, dreams (the oneiric dimension of experience), hypnosis and neuroses. The Freudian understanding of the psychopathology of everyday life is truly an impressive discovery. Even apart from the apparatus of a Freudian hermeneutic, the acknowledgement of the investment of the unconscious in our everydayness requires a multilayered architectural model of the experiencing self. Whether such a model suggests concrete manifestations of transcendent meanings depends upon the character of the unconscious investment in experience. In any case, unconscious mental processes constitute part of the topography of the self and thus constitute a layer of meaning which must be examined for sacred markings.

It is the work of Carl G. Jung that is most often associated with a positive valuation of the religious importance of unconscious contents. His work has come to be paradigmatic in relation to any further investigations of the parallelisms among the mythic, oneiric, and cosmic dimensions of experience. Jung's personal discovery of the unconscious is certainly one of the most important expeditions into the sacred dimensions of self realization. In fact, his autobiography, *Memories, Dreams, Reflections* is a catalogue of sacred markings. He almost exclusively focuses on those events in his life where the imperishable world of sacred times and sacred places interrupts the profane world of transitoriness and decay.[25]

Jung remembers the world of his childhood as having eternal qualities. The record of his childhood experiences documents his primary discovery of the sacred which is nourished and nuanced but not fundamentally changed by his passage into adulthood. These memories of early childhood are even more important than some of Jung's scientific reflections for discovering the world of religious meanings. Gaston Bachelard says that: "By dreaming on childhood, we return to the lair of reveries, to the reveries which have opened up the world to us."[26] What are some of these childhood reveries which have opened up the sacred world to sensitive observers? The eternality of childhood suggests the presence of universal motifs but they are always couched in the particularity of individual experience. Hence, Jung's memories are exemplary but not normative.

Childhood initiations into universal secrets and archetypal meanings are sacred markings in themselves and they are also clues to the characteristic appearance of sacred markings that are manifested in adult experience. For example, Jung suggests that his intellectual life had its unconscious beginnings in an initiatory dream which occurred between three and four years of age. The dream is itself a manifestation of the sacred, but more importantly, this dream is a matrix from which is cast further possibilities for the manifestation of the sacred.

The dream was of a subterranean ithyphallic God.[27] The ritual phallos was enthroned and Jung stood before it in fascination and in fear and trembling. The sacred revealed itself as creator and destroyer ("man eater"). For Jung there was no longer any possibility that God knew only the children of light. Sacred markings have their dark side and are often to be found in the shadows of life.

There are two other interesting childhood journeys into the sacred underworld recorded by Jung in his autobiography that shape the architectural model of the psyche in this elementary topography. The first is a complex relationship with a stone, a "soul stone." Jung played an imaginary game with a stone imbedded in the ground near the wall of the family garden. As he would sit on the stone the question would arise: "Am I the one who is sitting on the stone, or am I the stone on which *he* is sitting?" The question and the stone were shrouded in ambiguity. The stone like the ithyphallic God disclosed rumblings of chthonic forces that could not be clearly disconnected from the experience of self. Even as an adult, Jung sensed a primal connectedness with a reality imbedded in the earth as he stood on this mysterious stone.

The "soul stone" became an elaborated symbol in Jung's childhood world when he painted an oblong blackish stone from the Rhine so that it was divided into an upper and lower half. This stone was the secret property of a secret manikin which Jung had carved from his pencil case. He had long carried the stone in his pocket and it was now to be deposited with his manikin in a hiding place. Not only is the "soul stone" to be hidden with the secret person, but it is a symbol of the divided self. The "soul stone" was a source of life for the manikin. It revealed chthonic forces — a kratophany. He recognized that the bowels of the earth can be a depository of sacred meanings.

The experience of the divided self was not the early manifestation of a pathological situation. The dramatic interplay between surface experiences and subterranean experiences represented a natural individuation process. The "soul stone" symbolized the power to become whole without dissolving the multiplicity of meanings that belong to the self. Jung became aware of two not yet integrated sides of his personality. Throughout his school years he was schoolboy and an eighteenth century old man.[30] The old man was wise and made contact with the sacred. A phenomenology of sacred markings must pay close attention to the workings of the old man side of personal experience. This was all very confusing to Jung and it was not until he had a dream in which he was pursued by a gigantic black figure threatening to extinguish a small light in Jung's hands that Jung began to understand the relationship between his number one and number two personalities. The number one schoolboy personality was his consciousness lodged in the contemporary situation. Consciousness was a bearer of light. The number two personality was the shadow of the inner realm of light appearing to consciousness. The closure of childhood required that the number two personality now manifest itself in dreams. That is, the universal motifs belonging to childhood experience found residence in the shadowed reverie of night dreams.

The dream becomes a vehicle for expressing unconscious contents to the adult consciousness. Dreams can compensate for the limited vision imposed by consciousness and also disclose possibilities for future conscious realization. Dreams are a psychological adjustment to the exclusively conscious evaluation of the psyche.[31]

Two interesting dreams related by Jung constitute an oneiric unmasking of our psychic structure. The first of these dreams occurred on a journey to the United States on which Jung was accompanied by Sigmund Freud. Freud was unable to provide an interpretation of the dream which was satisfactory to Jung and thus the dream compensated for the Freudian vision of psychic dynamics. The dream took place in a two story house which was unfamiliar to Jung. He found himself in the opening of the dream on the second floor which was a kind of salon. When he descended to the ground floor he noticed that it was much older — probably dating back to the fifteenth or sixteenth century. As he continued to explore the house he went down into the cellar which was even older. The last descent took him into unknown depths in which there were artifacts that appeared to be the remains of a primitive culture. This dream revealed the multilayered structure of the psyche. Jung interpretively equated the salon with consciousness, the ground floor with a first layer of the unconscious and the successive floors as deeper layers of a collective psyche in which resides the primitive man in all of us.[32]

The second dream which reveals characteristics of the psychic structure coincided with Jung's investigations and increasing understanding of mandala symbolism. In the dream Jung was in *Liverpool*. It was dirty, night, winter, and raining. The city was arranged radially around a square in the center. In the square was a round pool and in the center of the pool was an island. All of the city was obscured with fog and darkness except for the island in the center. Jung's Swiss companions expressed surprise that another Swiss was living in Liverpool. Jung thought: "I know very well why he has settled here."[33]

Liverpool is the pool of life and Jung realized that this dream revealed that the goal of psychic dynamics is the centering process which gives us a vision of "unearthly," transcendent, beauty. He said, "Through this dream I understood that the self is the principle and archetype of orientation and meaning."[34]

The two dreams reveal several characteristics about the structure of the psyche that are particularly relevant in the search for sacred markings. The vision of transcendence is unobscured by darkness only at the center of self understanding. The self is shrouded by darkness so that one must pass through the darkness to reach the center. The center is a center because it is the point of convergence for many streets through the pool of life. The first dream suggests that this convergence is also a convergence of psychic layers giving a vertical as well as a horizontal dimension to the process of centering. The search for sacred markings must develop on a multiplicity of psychic levels and must not be afraid of inner city shadows that surround the center of self realization.

This does not mean that theology is to become only an interpretation of dreams. Even analytical psychology does not develop in this direction. Dreams are not viewed as the royal road to the unconscious.[35] According to Jung,[36] understanding the individuation process requires a knowledge of folklore, mythology and the history of religions. The dream has laid claim to the need for a complex view of the structure of the psyche that is immersed in religious meanings but it is not a sufficient modality in itself for the manifestation of sacred meanings. Veiled in the darkness of the night, dreams are intimations of sacred themes that can be clearly viewed only at the heart of the self, the center of *Liverpool*.

Since the union of conscious and unconscious material is necessary for viewing the self, vehicles must be developed so that the unconscious contents can be made available. Jung addressed himself to this problem in his essay "The Transcendent Function."[37] Dreams, parapraxes and neuroses are the obvious encounters with unconscious forces, but the first two examples usually are only fragmentary glimpses into the unconscious, and neuroses present unconscious contents only behind distorted masks. How can the theologian supplement his examination of unconscious contents? Since the psychology of the unconscious is not a wholly personal affair we find a residue of unconscious contents in the history of culture or more particularly in the history of religions and mythology. Unconscious contents have always been available to the theologian in the content of his own tradition. The connectedness of these contents with the immediate life of the contemporary religious community is an important aspect of the question addressed to theology concerning a need for a topography of sacred markings. Aside from understanding the parallelism that can be uncovered among the cosmic, oneiric, neurotic, dramatic, mythic, comic, and ludic dimensions of experience, Jung suggests that another complementary mode of contact with unconscious contents is through the development of an "active imagination." This method can be destructive and perhaps should not become a normal part of theological inquiry although the possibilities that it opens to theology are interesting and suggestive in the experiment of our life together. Free fantasizing through an "active imagination" sometimes allows for a more coherent presentation of unconscious contents. It is an exaggeration of the normal processes of bringing the realm of possibilities into consciousness through the establishment of contrasts. In this sense the possibility for free fantasizing and the ontological analogue to the "active imagination" is the transcendental imagination. Since all consciousness involves the conjunction of actuality and possibility, the method of "active imagination" is only a manifestation of the becoming of consciousness writ large. The "active imagination" can be viewed as a realization of the possibility for inner dialogue.

Jung gives a biographical example of the "active imagination" as a transcendent function in *Memories, Dreams, Reflections*.[38] Because of the bewildering presence of unfamiliar fantasy experiences in his encounter with unconscious contents, Jung found it necessary to construct an imaginary situation which gave him a controlled access to the unconscious. He imagined a steep descent and made several attempts to penetrate to the bottom of the chasm. Passing into a land of the dead with its other-worldly characteristics he made contact with archetypal figures which would guide and familiarize him with unconscious contents. The "active imagination" permitted entrance into deeper layers of psychic reality than were normally available outside of the dream experience.

The organization of materials from depth psychology into a structural model of the psyche does change the relief structure of the theologian's elementary topography of sacred markings. It is clear that he must look for hierophanies on the surfaces of mountains and valleys but he must also perform excavations below the surface of experience. The insights that Jung gleaned from his dreams of the psychic house and the psychic city become elaborated and clarified through his technical work. Here he develops his familiar multilayered model of the self. Of course, this model is not in itself a sacred marking. It is a functional tool for the growing discovery of sacred markings and it is an anticipation of the intelligibility of transcendent experiences. Thus depth psychology is an auxiliary to the method of foundational theology.

The model of the self in analytical psychology is an elaboration or magnification of our psychic landscape in a topography of sacred markings. This model and its use in a topography is a preliminary heuristic investigation into sacred meanings and it cannot be substituted for those meanings. Since the model of the self in analytical psychology is an anticipation of sacred markings, it thereby reinforces the naive openness of immediate consciousness to elementary hierophanies. This second naivete is a variation of the phenomenological epoche.

The radical shift in Jung's conception of the self from the psychoanalytic model of the self appears when he posits the coexistence of a secondary psychic system which is collective and universal alongside of the personal individualistic conscious psychic system with its personalized unconscious correlates. This view is beyond the boundaries of ego psychology because the self does not equal the ego.[39] The ego complex is the center of the field of consciousness and emerges out of the history of conscious behavior. The self has already been encountered in the oneiric images from Jung's autobiographical reflections. It was characterized as diversely layered but yet also depicted as a composite whole in mandala figures. These were images of the structure and dynamic inter-relation of the primary and secondary psychic systems.

There are three distinguishable layers of happenings in the analytical model of the self. On the surface of experience is consciousness. The ego complex is identified with the center of conscious experience. Below the surface is a superficial layer of unconscious happenings called the personal unconscious. The contents of the personal unconscious are feeling-toned complexes which have been determined by vicissitudes of personal experience. The deepest layer of unconscious happenings is collective and universal. The contents of the collective unconscious are the archetypes or primordial forms.[40] The notion of the collective psyche does not pretend to be an ontological description, but in fact the concept of the archetypes of the collective unconscious is a psychological rendering of a metaphysical theme expressed in the Platonic realm of ideas, Whitehead's realm of eternal objects, forms for the specific determination of facts, or the transcendental notion of a realm of possibilities. The secondary psychic system transcends the limitations of personal history and discloses the universal realm of possibility. The integration of the primary and secondary psychic systems is thus a conjunction of actuality and possibility. This is the process of individuation according to Jung and it is also the elementary definition of transcendence developed for this inquiry. The psychology of individuation is a psychology of *homo religiosus*.

Jung even suggests that Christ exemplifies the archetype of the self.[41] He claims that Christological formulae are the nearest analogy to the self and its meaning. The envisagement of the Christ as wholly God and wholly man in perfect union is an envisagement of the self as a coincidence of opposites. The realization of the self and the understanding of the Christ-event share many of the same characteristics. The individuation process brings together the universal and the particular, the eternal and the temporal, male and female, heaven and earth, the collective and the personal, good and evil. When the orthodox Christological formulations fail to complete the union of opposites embodied in the archetype of the self, Jung turns to gnostic literature or medieval alchemy to see the transformation of the Christ-event into a balanced principle of individuation. The archetype of the self is alternatively expressed by other soteriological concepts such as the Atman-Brahman synthesis in the Indian experience.

The dramatic quest for self realization has religious expression because it is a religious event. When the dramatic rendering of experience no longer contains sacred markings it often contains neurotic markings. Jung has sometimes said to his older patients: "Your picture of God or your idea of immortality is atrophied; consequently your psychic metabolism is out of gear."[42] The dramatic dimensions of religious meanings are then expressed *via negativa* through the grips of neurosis.

Psychopathological expressions, neurotic or psychotic, within experience are frequently intertwined with religious motifs or symbol systems. In this inquiry we are not so much interested in determining the casual relationships that exist between religion and psychopathology, as recognizing their complicity in each other. Freud writes that neurosis is an individual religiosity and religion is a universal neurosis. Religion and neurosis imitate each other.[43] Jung feels that in the last analysis the fundamental problem of all of his patients in the latter stages of their lives is that they did not have a healthy religious outlook.[44] These opposing evaluations of the relationship between religion and neurosis at least jointly suggest that there is a fundamental relationship between neurotic dimensions of experience and religion. In a topography of sacred markings the nature of the relationship remains indeterminant and is subordinate to recognizing the fact of the relationship. The neurotic personality is not a manifestation of the sacred; but even this caricature of individuation processes cannot disguise the fact that man is *homo religiosus*.

III

The segregation of seven areas of experiencing from the whole process of individuation is an artificial separation. None of these dimensions can be isolated from each other or from the everyday rhythm of secular experience. The importance of an elementary topography of sacred markings has been to demonstrate that imbedded within the everydayness of experience are manifestations of an otherness that condition life and need to be incorporated into any evaluation of personhood.

An elementary topography of sacred markings also demonstrates that the sacred manifests itself outside of the walls of the sanctuary. In fact, the importance of religious understanding depends upon the fact that sacred meanings are coextensive with the full range of experiencing. The church is an institution and it is more than an institution. Foundational theology extends the conception of the church beyond any artificial boundaries of piety. Once again it appears that the church is best understood as a universal communion of possibility.

NOTES

1. See Wilfred Cantwell Smith, *The Meaning and End of Religion* (New York: New American Library, Mentor Books, 1964), p. 165. "My particular hypothesis here is that religious statements express the faith of persons, who as persons are involved in transcendence."
2. Bernard Lonergan, *Insight: A Study of Human Understanding* (New York: Philosophical Library, Revised Student's Edition, 1958) p. 635.
3. Langdon Gilkey, *Naming the Whirlwind: The Renewal of God Language* (Indianapolis: Bobbs-Merrill, 1969), pp. 248-255.
4. Mircea Eliade and J. Kitagawa, eds., *The History of Religions* (Chicago: University of Chicago Press, 1959), pp. 24, 88.
5. Gilkey, *Naming the Whirlwind,* p. 10.
6. Peter Berger, *A Rumor of Angels* (Garden City, New York: Doubleday Anchor Books, 1970), p. 24.
7. Paul Ricoeur, *Freud and Philosophy: An Essay in Interpretation* (New Haven: Yale University Press, 1970), pp. 14-15; and Paul Ricoeur, *The Symbolism of Evil* (New York: Harper and Row, 1967), pp. 10-14.
8. The recognition of these multiple dimensions of experience is widespread and is found in writings of Harvey Cox, Sam Keen, Peter Berger, Paul Tillich, Bernard Lonergan, *et al.*
9. Peter Berger, *The Precarious Vision* (Garden City, N.Y.: Doubleday, 1961), p. 207; and *The Rumor of Angels,* p. 69.
10. See Johan Huizinga, *Homo Ludens: A Study of the Play Element in Culture* (Boston Beacon Press, 1955), pp. 8, 11, 12.
11. Berger, *A Rumor of Angels,* p. 58.

12. Nathan Scott, *The Broken Center* (New Haven: Yale University Press, 1966), p. 4.
13. Martin Heidegger, *Existence and Being* (Chicago: Regnery Gateway Edition, 1965), p. 282.
14. Ricoeur, *Freud and Philosophy*, p. 15. (Italics mine.)
15. Ivan Svitak, *Man and His World: A Marxian View* (New York: Dell Publishing Co., 1970), p. 121. This has dramatic humanizing consequences for Svitak's concept of man. He says, "it (the poem) conceals within itself an essential side of man." p. 117.
16. Nathan Scott, *Negative Capability* (New Haven: Yale University Press, 1969), p. 94.
17. Martin Heidegger, *On the Way to Language* (New York: Harper and Row, 1971), p. 192.
18. See Mircea Eliade, *The Quest* (Chicago: University of Chicago Press, 1969), Chapter 1, especially p. 10.
19. Quote is from Lonergan, *Insight*, p. 187.
20. Sam Keen, *To A Dancing God* (New York: Harper and Row, 1970), p. 86.
21. Cf. James Lynwood Walker, *Body and Soul* (Nashville: Abingdon Press, 1971), pp. 33-36, 49-55.
22. Maurice Merleau-Ponty, *The Phenomenology of Perception* (London: Routledge & Kegan Paul, 1962), p. 82.
23. Charles Brenner, *An Elementary Textbook of Psychoanalysis* (Garden City, N.Y.: Doubleday Anchor Book, 1957), p. 2.
24. Sigmund Freud, *A General Introduction to Psychoanalysis* (New York: Washington Square Press, 1968), p. 25. (Italics mine.)
25. Carl Jung, *Memories, Dreams, Reflections* (New York: Random House Vintage Books, 1963), p. 4.
26. Gaston Bachelard, *The Poetics of Reverie* (New York: Grossman Publishing Inc., 1969), p. 102.
27. For a full account of the dream see Jung, *Memories, Dreams, Reflections*, pp. 11-12.
28. *Ibid.*, p. 20.
29. *Ibid.*, p. 21.
30. *Ibid.*, pp. 30-90.
31. See Carl Jung, *Collected Works Vol. 8* (New York: Bollingen Foundation, 2nd Edition, 1969), pp. 237-280, for a discussion of the compensatory and prospective function of dreams.
32. Jung, *Memories, Dreams, Reflections*, pp. 168-171.
33. *Ibid.*, pp. 197-198.
34. *Ibid.*, p. 199.
35. Jolande Jacobi, *Complex, Archetype, Symbol* (New York: Bollingen Foundation, 1959), p. 6; or Jung, *Collected Works Vol. 8*, p. 101.
36. Jung, *Collected Works Vol. 8*, p. 290.
37. *Ibid.*, pp. 67-91.
38. Jung, *Memories, Dreams, Reflections*, p. 181.
39. Carl Jung, *Collected Works Vol. 9ii* (New York: Bollingen Foundation, 2nd edition, 1970), pp. 3, 5.
40. Carl Jung, *Collected Works Vol. 9i* (New York: Bollingen Foundation, 2nd edition, 1971), pp. 3, 4.
41. See Jung, *Collected Works Vol. 9ii*, pp. 36-71.
42. Carl Jung, *Modern Man in Search of a Soul* (New York: Harcourt, Brace and World Harvest Books, 1933), p. 113.
43. Ricoeur, *Freud and Philosophy*, p. 232.
44. Jung, *Modern Man in Search of a Soul*, p. 229.

CHAPTER VI

SACRED MARKINGS II:
LIMITS AND DISTORTIONS

he conception of a theological mapping of sacred markings on the contours of experience is actually determined by the range of secular understanding. As we have seen, sacred markings are not in fact co-extensive with elementary acts of transcendence but represent the range of experiences in which the dimensions of ''otherness'' that accompany transcendence have enough intensity and enormity to cross into the threshold of consciousness. The range of consciousness is not a religious phenomenon but is determined by secular expectations of intelligibility. Thus an elementary topography of sacred markings is more of an analysis of culture than an analysis of the word of God. The topography of sacred markings is the church's theological self-conscousness of being in a secular world. It is a reflection of theology's understanding of its shared responsibility with the physical and social sciences for rendering life intelligible.

I

The second part of our discussion of sacred markings is an attempt to understand the meaning of paradigm limits in theology and the sciences as it is related to our understanding of the hermeneutical task. The use of images of depth and transcendence at the frontiers of paradigm utility raises two separate questions. The hermeneutical question concerns the direct interpretation of frontier language or imagery. The foundational theological question concerns the structures and limits of paradigm use-fulness which underlie the concept of frontiers and the structures of knowing which take us into frontier experiences. Since we have already turned to ontological dimensions in knowing, this chapter's response to the foundational questions will be a discussion of paradigm limits and concrete manifestations of knowing acts.

The recognition of paradigm limits is an achievement of the historian and philosopher of science more than an achievement of the theologian and philosopher of religion. Because of upheaval and transition, the physical sciences have become self conscious of themselves and are exemplary for the understanding of disciplinary integrity and disciplinary limits. Thus, the philosophy of science is directly related to the question of the relationship between theological studies and scientific studies in a topography of sacred markings but also provides a model for understanding paradigm formation and paradigm limits. In particular, I think that the significant recasting of the scientific model found in the related works of Thomas S. Kuhn, Stephen Toulmin, and Michael Polanyi is an important tool for cultural analysis in foundational theology.[1]

Kuhn claims that when we examine the *historical* record of the research activity of science there emerges a decisive transformation in our understanding of the nature of science. Most importantly, the philosophy of science has overestimated observation in the process of discovery. Einstein has criticized both Newton and his followers for the naive belief that the basic concepts of their physical system could be derived from experience. They did not comprehend the place of ''mind'' in the creation of scientific concepts.[2] The need for a reinterpretation of the nature of science developed out of the realization both in relativity physics and in the philosophy of science that a scientific theory is not a collection of facts but, in a very profound sense, the creation of order.

Kuhn believes that it is the pedagogic form which has misled us in our search for an adequate concept of science.[3] The textbook image of science upon which we nurture young scientists presents scientific activity as a series of questions and answers. After filling out several workbooks the student would naturally begin to understand science as the piecemeal accumulation of facts. Scientific creativity is overshadowed by past scientific achievements. The student can be introduced to the models or paradigms which govern the normal research activities of scientists but he cannot be taught the genius of creativity in theoretical science. The philosopher of science, however, must recognize both the normal and theoretical activities of scientists in his conceptualization of science. It is the theoretical scientist who determines the disciplinary limits of his science and it is thus the work of the theoretical scientist that is of most interest to foundational theology. The normal scientist accepts the theoretical paradigm and devotes his research to the range of problems laid bare by the paradigm.

According to Kuhn, theoretical science is concerned with the creation of paradigms which determine the limits and expectations of intelligibility for normal scientific research. Theoretical science is a synthetic process always moving toward novelty. It is debated but certainly undecided whether or not there is any logic of creativity in theoretical science. Polanyi is convinced that the actual event of discovery or creativity is "a process of spontaneous mental reorganization uncontrolled by conscious effort."[4] In any case, it appears that the work of theoretical scientist bears a closer kinship with the work of the artist than with the work of the engineer. The creation of a paradigm is the foundation of a science and is not itself the object of the science as determined by the paradigm. Understanding the creativity of science is the proper object of transcendental inquiry. Knowing that the paradigm is a creation of theoretical science unmasks pretensions of ultimacy and immutability that have sometimes been mistakenly attributed to scientific inquiry.

It is actually the successes of the research activity of normal scientists that have misled many commentators on the history of scientific advance. Too frequently, the puzzle-solving successes of normal science have been inflated in importance and thereby confuse serious assessments of the dimensions of theoretical science.

The activity of normal science begins with paradigm acceptance. The understanding of the paradigm is the foundation for acceptance into the community of normal scientific research, the foundation for communication within the community, and the foundation for research itself. Paradigm limits are the limits for research within the accepted community of scientific practitioners. It is the community that gives paradigm status to a theory. The community of practitioners actualizes normal science. Paradigm truth is the decision of a community and not an endowment from nature. Both the nature of the community and the governing paradigm introduce the concepts of limits into the conceptualization of science. These limits regulate the activity of normal science and in this sense have expression in the frustrations of normal science confounded by dimensions of unexpected experiences which transgress the boundaries of intelligibility. That which lies beyond the limits of an accepted paradigm is characterized by dimensions of "otherness."

The encounter with the familiar and expected in normal science is part of the "mopping up" operation at the core of normal research.[5] The first concern of normal science is fact gathering, the observing and recording of phenomena. Fact gathering is very selective. Fact gathering is dependent on the paradigm's determination of what is significant. The foundation for this decision cannot be derived from the facts themselves. Observation is conditioned by the paradigm learning process which is prerequisite to admission into the scientific community. This way the community is not bothered by irrelevant details.

The second activity of normal science which seems to be misleading to outside observers is the verification of predictions predicated upon the paradigm. The scientist verifies the paradigm by comparing the predictions with newly observed data. The significance of the newly observed data is determined by the accepted paradigm. New observations increase the statistical probability that the paradigm is adequate by increasing the quantity of data which originally gave credibility to the paradigm.

A third concern of the normal scientist is the articulation of the paradigm. Within the structure of scientific revolutions this is certainly the most important direction for normal scientific research. Three more divisions are possible within this group. (1) The determination of constants implied in the paradigm is important to paradigm articulation. It is absolutely essential for verification and application of the paradigm. The novelty it seeks is not theoretical. The constant is already implied in the paradigm. (2) Another very important aspect of paradigm articulation is the determination of scientific laws within the paradigm. The paradigm is necessary for such discoveries as Charles' law or Boyle's law. (3) The most productive and expansive form of paradigm articulation is paradigm application. What this means is that the applicability of the paradigm is experimentally tried in different situations outside of the domain of its original or common applications. Of the three forms of paradigm articulation, paradigm application most resembles exploration.[6]

Research in normal science does not aim at the development of new paradigms. It does not aim at conceptual novelty. Kuhn says that normal science is a puzzle-solving activity and that it is the challenge of the puzzle which satisfies the scientist in his work. With the help of the paradigm the normal scientist chooses a problem that only a lack of ingenuity or poor laboratory techniques should keep him from finding a solution.[7]

Normal science does not aim at novelty but its researches often disclose an unexpected novelty. If this novelty is not comprehended by the community's accepted paradigm, Kuhn refers to it as an anomaly. The anomaly can be ignored; the paradigm can be expanded to comprehend the anomaly although often in an ad hoc manner; or, the anomaly can be understood as a counter-instance to the paradigm. If the anomaly is a counter-instance we must demand a paradigm shift and experience a scientific revolution.

It is only against backgrounds of crisis that novel theories emerge in science. It is only after pronounced failure in the normal problem solving activity that the time is ready for change. Before the Copernican revolution took concrete form, the Ptolemaic system was a scandal. It was both cumbersome and inaccurate. Before the emergence of the theory of relativity, classical physics was in a dilemma. The problem about ether drift and the unwarranted assumptions as to an inertial coordinate system appeared as irresponsible to theoretical scientists of extraordinary vision. Even in the seventeenth century Leibniz criticized Newton's conception of an absolute inertial coordinate system.[8]

Against this background of crisis an anomaly not only stands outside of the scope of a paradigm but stands over against it as a counter-instance refuting the validity of the paradigm's application. The problem falls outside of the realm of normal research. Normal science does not remain oblivious to the problem, but, since the solution lies in the creation of an alternative paradigm, the process must be referred to the extraordinary or theoretical activity of the scientist.

The activity of the normal scientist is predicated upon the activity of the theoretical scientist. Paradigm failure concretely refers us back to the work of the theoretical scientist as the foundation of normal science. Thus the paradigms of theoretical scientists are the justification and foundation of meaning for the work of normal scientists. It is the theoretical paradigm that assigns concrete meaning to the concept of limits. Paradigm anticipations of intelligibility contain their own limits but cannot go beyond these limits. The foundations of a paradigm lie outside of the limits of its application. Thus, the paradigm cannot be its own foundation nor can there be an appeal to the absoluteness of experience as its foundation. The paradigm determines the meaningfulness of experience and thereby relativizes the role of experience in determining the meaningfulness of a paradigm.

Every scientific paradigm is surrounded by limiting questions. The upper limits of the paradigm are determined by the meaning of intelligibility fixed by the heuristic structures internal to the paradigm and the lower limits of the paradigm are determined by its natural inability to justify its own foundations. The one time astounding claim of mathematican Kurt Gödel that the axiomatic method has certain inherent limitations which deny the possibility that even the arithmetic of integers can be fully axiomatized is now paralleled by the familiar claim of the philosopher of science that all paradigmatic systems have internal limitations.[9] An alternative language which lies outside of the scope of the paradigm must be used to thematize the movement toward paradigm foundations. The language by which we can explicate paradigm foundations is a language of possibility, the possibility for the paradigm. It is a language of elementary transcendence in which possibility for the articulation of order is conjoined with the actuality of experience.

Elementary acts of transcendence appear as dimensions of "otherness" at the limits of paradigm adequacy and mark regions of religio-mythic symbolism. Even if scientific language is used beyond the boundaries of scientific inquiry it is used symbolically and constitutes a dimension of mythology.[10] This is not an argument against science or for religion. It is the recognition that the determination of place for the elementary consciousness of sacred markings is proportionate to the scope of secular self-consciousness. The characteristic appearance of the horizon is determined by the point of perspective taken by the observer and the loci for limiting questions is a function of secular consciousness. A topography of sacred markings is thoroughly relativized by the historical situation in which it is charted.

The importance of transcendence cannot be thoroughly assessed through the analysis of sacred markings. The existence of sacred markings bears witness to the presence of transcendent meanings throughout experience but in themselves they are more of a reflection on the limits of cultural achievements than a revelation of God. The maximum field of vision for a fully developed scientific or philosophical model can only be a penultimate vision. An ultimate vision is a function of transcendent knowledge achievable only when we have the complete set of answers to the complete set of questions.[11] Only an act of unrestricted understanding establishes a limit to the concepts of limits and transcendence.

The concept of paradigm limits has essential religious meaning when the relative historical expressions of transcendence are interpreted in the context of an unrestricted desire to know. The relativity of a topography of concrete markings issues in the call for an analysis of an ultimate horizon under which all preliminary horizons are subsumed. In this case horizon fusion is actually a transcendence of penultimate limits. Limits on the range of paradigm application do not correspond with limits imposed on the desire to know. In fact, the recognition of boundaries or limits to any given patterns of intelligibility is usually accompanied by a question concerning what lies beyond these boundaries or limits.

There is no limit that cannot be called into question except the limiting concept of all limits, the complete set of answers to the complete set of questions. Only such a hypothetical act of unrestricted understanding can assign a limit to the concept of transcendence.[12] The unrestricted desire to know requires a symbolic language to thematically express its own goal since it remains unrealized in the content of our intellectual achievements. In this case, a topography of sacred markings determines the locus of a horizon which lies beyond the achievable contents of human understanding. The horizon which is not a function of our own cultural limitations, which is not a function of our fallibility, and which is not a function of our perversity is a cipher of transcendence empty of any intellectual content.

The unrestricted desire to know is experienced as a question posed to existence. It is first experienced as an elementary step of transcendence in what may appear as simple questions.[13] Questioning contains its own radical foundation. It is impossible to call into question our ability to question. The inability to assign anything but a practical limit on questioning pushes the desire to know beyond paradigm restrictions. The ability to question is a function of what we are and it is not contained by paradigm limits. Only the content of questioning and the anticipations of intelligibility are shaped by existing paradigms. But, since paradigms themselves can be called into question, the limits of questioning are always existential choices. The choice can remain open.

A topography of sacred markings has come to focus on a dialectic between the act and content of knowing. The content of knowing is subject to paradigm limits but the act of knowing is subject only to the limits assigned to questioning by the self.

There is never a sense in which finite acts of understanding can objectively determine the content of an ultimate reality or the character of an ultimate horizon. Lonergan's conception of transcendent being as the complete set of answers to the complete set of questions is a notation for ultimate reality and not a revelation of that reality. Out of this conception there is no content to be proclaimed. Transcendent being makes a claim upon acts of understanding but does not here become a content for understanding. Thus, understanding understanding requires a language of transcendence and secular understanding does not secure that language for itself. A topography of sacred markings leads us to agree with Gilkey that the most serious challenge to a purely secular understanding of secular existence is that it cannot provide for itself a language or symbolism capable of expressing or thematizing the meaning and possibilities of its own nature.[14] This is also why a topography of sacred markings and even more sophisticated phenomenological investigations of secular consciousness are only prologomena to dogmatic theology.

II

Calvin says in the *Institutes of the Christian Religion* that "There is within the human mind, and indeed by natural instinct, an awareness of divinity."[15] It is this knowledge and sensitivity to dimensions of ultimacy that justifies the conception of a topography of sacred markings as prologomena to theology. However, Calvin continues by claiming that "This knowledge is either smothered or corrupted, partly by ignorance, partly by malice."[16] Recognizing the fallibility and perversity of the intellect restricts the expansion of a topography of sacred markings from growth into a natural theology or its use as a substitute for the gospel.

The preceding analysis of paradigm limits is a secular investigation of the fallibility of the intellect. Every scientific, philosophical, or even theological paradigm is internally limited and cannot be substituted for the word of God. Paradigms are useful and even necessary accompaniments for interpreting the word of God but they cannot be equated with absolute truth. Paradigm limits are manifestations of our finite capacity to think. They are manifestations of fallibility.

Expressions of the perversity of the intellect are more carefully hidden and are often masked with pretensions of certainty. Not only is it impossible for fallible man to fully grasp the reality of the ultimate, but perverse man chooses against grasping toward dimensions of ultimacy in human experience. With double disguise, man chooses to ignore signals of transcendence in the world, and then chooses to hide the reality of his choice. The flight from understanding and the resultant eclipse of knowledge are special problems that question the possibility and viability of a topography of sacred markings.

The dark side of the psychoanalytic contribution to theology appears. In the elementary topography of sacred markings both psychoanalysis and analytic psychology provided images of transcendence in the dramatic, oneiric, and neurotic passage through life. These regions of experiencing are zones for the emergence of symbolism precisely because man is capable of expressing himself and realizing his desires symbolically. Psychoanalytic research has shown, however, that symbols can mask desires as well as reveal meanings. Ricoeur notes in his monumental study of Freud that the multivalence of symbols containing the possibility for disclosure as well as masking requires a dipolar interpretation of interpretation. A hermeneutics of expansion is committed to the restoration of meaning and a hermeneutics of suspicion is committed to a reduction of illusion.[17] A hermeneutics of expansion is a response to our fallibility; a hermeneutics of suspicion is a response to our perversity.

The possibility of disguise in the overdetermination of symbols undermines the adequacy of self reflection as the fundamental tool in the development of a topography of sacred markings. The phenomenological interpretation of sacred markings is a mixed discourse of repression and revelation. The dispossession of consciousness by psychoanalytic theory as the sole arbiter of meaning gives an antiphenomenological bias to a hermeneutics of suspicion. The psychoanalytic relocation of meaning in an unconscious over which we exercise little control widens the gap between the promise and fulfillment of understanding transcendence through extrapolations from experience in the development of a purely secular theology.

Thus, transcendence appears but is not understood on the boundaries of paradigm usefulness. The fully developed meaning of transcendence is hidden and the sacred marking is really a function of paradigm limitations. But, this experience of finitude is complicated by the repression of meaning. The natural desire to move toward a horizon of unrestricted understanding can be deflected by fears of inadequacy. The desire to know is then masked in pretensions of absolute knowledge or superior understanding.

The experience of transcendence manifested in the failure of a paradigm is sometimes disguised as the experience of transcendence manifested as a paradigm achievement. The paradigm is then positively invested with meanings that go beyond it. The resulting overvaluation of the paradigm is used to repress questions that cross the boundaries of paradigm application. The elementary act of transcendence internal to the intellectual pattern of experience is repressed. What appears to be reverence for the sacred is actually a disguise for failure and becomes an obstruction to elementary transcendent acts. This form of obscurantism is familiar to those who live within the institutional church. It is also familiar to the scientific community when reverence for "scientific method" is substituted for reverence for the sacred.

The failure of scientific and philosophical paradigms on the boundaries of paradigm usefulness can also lead to an undervaluation of paradigm formation as an intellectual tool and thus support another form of obscurantism. When paradigm formation is circumscribed by narrow positivistic boundaries, questions that cross these narrow boundaries enforced by positivism are brushed aside as meaningless. In other words, elementary acts of transcendence are brushed aside as meaningless. The unimaginative routine mind mistakes familiarity of the ordinary with security. Philosophical speculation is curtailed in the interest of philosophy. This flight from understanding is masked as a flight from ambiguity when in fact it is a flight from transcendence.

III

The recognition of paradigm limits and distortions is a secondary reflection on the meaning and importance of an elementary topography of sacred markings. What began as a "rumor of angels" remains as a "rumor of angels," albeit an expanded and chastened "rumor of angels."

In summation there are several considerations that should be restated. First, a topography of sacred markings is primarily an examination of the limits of secular consciousness and secular understanding. The boundaries of paradigm expansion mark the inadequacies of secular consciousness to express its own significance and illuminate a context for meaning. The elementary acts of transcendence that approach and cross paradigm limits remain unintelligible. A place, but not a content, for the proclamation of sacred meanings has been determined. The elementary acts of transcendence that make secular understanding possible are a judgment on the content of secular understanding. Religious understanding is necessary to rescue secular experience.

Secondly, a topography of sacred markings is subject to distortions introduced by choices, sometimes unconscious choices, against understanding. This means that a topography of sacred markings can only be provisional. A topography of sacred markings is not a natural theology. It is a preliminary inquiry fraught with many difficulties and dangers for the interpretation of religious meaning.

Thirdly, the positive significance of a topography of sacred markings is a function of the negative significance of such a map. Because the topography raises questions that it does not answer, we are underway toward a larger horizon. The analysis of questioning suggests that this horizon is the ultimate horizon of being. The topography prepares the way for an encounter with the word of God. The topography is a provisional valuation of religious symbolism. The topography of sacred markings is a reflection on the incompleteness of secular understanding without access to religious language and symbolism.

Fourthly, dimensions of transcendence revealed in dramatic, poetic, comic, ludic, cosmic, oneiric and neurotic regions are only ambiguously present to secular understanding. This suggests that self understanding is a primary function of religious understanding. The threshold of satisfaction for the integration of self understanding is extended beyond the limits of secular psychology into a psychology of *homo religiosus* by a topography of sacred markings. The sacred has entered into the definition of human life. The sacred will always appear even on the boundaries of a highly developed secular understanding of life because the sacred is at the center of human experience. A hermeneutic of the word of God is existential because essentially men and women are hearers of that word.

Notes

1. The historical rendering of this new conception of science is best expressed in Thomas S. Kuhn, *The Structure of Scientific Revolutions* (Chicago: University of Chicago Press, Phoenix Edition, 1964).
2. Edward H. Madden, ed., *The Structure of Scientific Thought* (Boston: Houghton Mifflin Co., 1960), p. 82.
3. Kuhn, p. 142.
4. Michael Polanyi, *Science, Faith and Society* (Chicago: University of Chicago Press, Phoenix Edition, 1964), p. 34.
5. Kuhn, p. 24.
6. *Ibid.*, pp. 25-34.
7. *Ibid.*, pp. 35-37.
8. Max Jammer, *Concepts of Space* (Cambridge, Mass.: Harvard University Press, 1954), pp. 114-124.
9. Ernest Nagel and James R. Newman, *Gödel's Proof* (New York: New York University Press, 1958), p. 6.
10. See Langdon Gilkey, *Religion and the Scientific Future* (New York: Harper and Row, 1970), pp. 37-40.
11. For an impressive development of this suggestion see Bernard Lonergan, *Insight: A Study of Human Understanding* (New York: Philosophical Library, Revised Student's Edition, 1958), Chpt. XIX.
12. *Ibid.*, p. 643.
13. cf. *Ibid.*, p. 635.
14. Langdon Gilkey, *Naming the Whirlwind: The Renewal of God-Language* (Indianapolis: Bobbs-Merrill Co., 1969), p. 250.
15. John Calvin, *Institutes of the Christian Religion,* 2 vols. (Philadelphia: Westminster Press, Library of Christian Classics Vol. XX, 1960), p. 43.
16. *Ibid.*, p. 47.
17. Paul Ricoeur, *Freud and Philosophy: An Essay on Interpretation* (New Haven: Yale University Press, 1970), p. 27.

CHAPTER VII

THE HERMENEUTIC
OF THE
WORD OF GOD

A secular topography of sacred markings cannot come to completion. An interpretation of sacred markings, a hermeneutic of the word of man, is internally limited to provisional horizons and is also subject to disguise and distortion.

The question, "How do things stand in being?", which defines the quest for intelligibility, necessarily remains unanswered when it is circumscribed by the provisional horizons of secular understanding. A secular topography of sacred markings exhausts itself or becomes empty of content as it pursues an absolute horizon. Karl Jasper's term "ciphers of transcendence" is uniquely appropriate to indicate that a pure transcendence does not itself have phenomenality.[1] Although ciphers are sometimes equated with the symbols of a secret code, a cipher also means to be empty, a naught, a zero. Ciphers are realities in our experience but they are not embodied tranendence.[2] They mark the reality of transcendence. They are sacred markings but they are not identical with sacrality. Ciphers of transcendence illuminate the limits of provisional grounds and provisional horizons against the claims of transcendence but they do not hold a content of transcendence.

Transcendence has been identified with the simple raising of questions in an intellectual pattern of experience, but the meaning of transcendence cannot be assessed until we move to the horizon of questions, the complete set of answers to the complete set of questions. This is the horizon of being. The philosophical interpretation of hermeneutics has witnessed to the overwhelming significance of the complicity between being and language in the movement to an ultimate horizon. Consciousness is dependent upon a word-event and the word-event is an ontological contrast of actuality and possibility. The otherness of possibility determines the meaning and consciousness of actuality but cannot itself become conscious except in the dialectical movement in which its own ingression into realization is contrasted with a larger possibility. The horizon of possibility remains opaque to the consciousness of actuality. The foundations of consciousness in contrast and limitation regulate the expansion of metaphysical inquiry so that it can never make intelligible the horizon of being. Only the limits of provisional horizons can be transcended and contrasted with the presence of new possibilities. The metaphysical possibilities for a dialectic of transcendence is a function of conditioned realization and always puts us underway toward new horizons. These new horizons illumine new regions of experiencing but do not exhaust the possibility for new experiences. Provisional horizons are a function of limits and a marking of transcendence. Metaphysics cannot complete itself because its achievements are actually its limitations.

There is a phenomenological analogue to the discovery of limits in metaphysical inquiry within the development of a topography of sacred markings. This secular inquiry into the meaning of transcendence is a discernment of the effective but limited range of paradigm application. Secular inquiry discovers the impossibility of containing the meaning of possibility within a provisional horizon. The drive of limitless concern penetrates beyond horizon limits with the raising of the simple question concerning the nature of the horizon itself. Once the horizon is itself called into question, it ceases to be the horizon under which the inquiry proceeds.

A topography of sacred markings is a valorization of transcendence without being an understanding of transcendence. We know that there are possibilities and meanings which have not been realized. There is now reason to listen for the word of God. The frustration of entering the hermeneutical circle that claims that we must understand in order to believe has been minimized. Precritical belief in the content of religious proclamation is supplanted by a belief in the meaningfulness of the act of proclamation. We become hearers of the word of God because we have heard the word of man and have discerned its limits.

The secular theology of a topography of sacred markings is a negative theology. The secular theologian can announce that the meaning of transcendence has become lost to modern man or that God is dead, but he cannot preach a "good news." This negativity of secular theology is certainly not to be interpreted as nihilism. Secular theology can announce the longing for a fullness of transcendence as well as recognize the incompleteness or provisional characteristics of secular models of intelligibility. A negative theology is a preparation for a positive theology that can then speak from within the hermeneutical circle. What I have been calling negative theology is in fact a positive foundation for understanding the possibilities for being hearers of the word of God.

I

The actual movement from negative theology to positive theology is not an achievement of negative theology. As Karl Rahner has suggested in *Hearers of the Word,* positive theology exists not because man thinks but because God has spoken.[3] It is not the incompleteness of secular thought forms but the fullness of God's address that is the primary datum for the development of a positive theology.

Foundational theology penetrates into the meaning of symbolism but does not create new symbols. The topography of sacred markings focused upon regions of experience in which transcendence was as meaningfully absent as it was present. Foundational theology poses a radical question to existence that reaches beyond every provisional horizon. Foundational theology is an intellectual elaboration of the prophetic principle that protests the apotheosis of provisional or conditioned aspects of life.

Through a topography of sacred markings we have discerned the presence of the sacred in the judgments of possibility upon actuality and in the need to transcend the limits of secular models of understanding. The sacred has been given unique value through the recognition of finite and conditioned intellectual paradigms as finite and conditioned. Thus, foundational theology prevents the usurpation of ultimate meanings by provisional and conditioned realities. This is, in effect, an application of the protestant principle that justification is by grace through faith With relation to ultimate meanings, God alone can act. We are claimed by God and no human or religious claim can bind God.[4]

The protestant principle is not a sufficient ground for the development of positive theology. It prepares the way for viewing God's action in history. The substance of positive theology is given to experience and is not derived from experience. It cannot be derived from experience. Positive theology exists because the presence of the sacred given to a community gives the occasion for thought.[5] With continuing reference to the phenomenological studies of Paul Ricoeur, we recognize that a symbol, part of the primary language of confession, gives rise to thought. But, in accordance with the meaning and importance of the protestant principle, we also recognize that the word of God is neither discovered nor created by man but is given to thought by God.

Positive theology is actually rooted in the significance of the twofold claim that the fundamental confession of Christianity is given to us and that it gives rise to thought. Theology proceeds with a given proclamation that continues to give. The basic Christian confession that begins with the certaintly of the proclamation of Jesus that "the Kingdom of God is beginning, is beginning now," and continues to claim the life of the Christian with the witness that "Christ is risen" gives rise to thought; it gives rise to positive theology. Thus, we are in agreement with Ebeling that the starting point for a positive development can be the certainty that the word of God has entered language.[7] Theology is possible because God has broken the silence by speaking. The unique symbols that call a positive Christian theology into existence are given in the proclamation of the word of God.

The meaning of the claim that symbols are given to Christian thought can be clarified by examining characteristics of the teachings of Jesus. New Testament scholars have said that the teachings of Jesus are to be understood as proclamation rather than as philosophical or apocalyptic speculation. The action of God is not an object of reflection.[8] Jesus does not offer an alternative philosophy. Jesus is the bearer of the word of God and not words about God. The proclamation of Jesus is an eschatological gospel and as such is also an eschatological event.[9] The word of God that Jesus proclaims is a word of forgiveness, a word of acceptance.[10] According to Jeremias, "The good news consists in the fact that Jesus invites sinners to God's festive meal."[11] Such an invitation cannot be confused with philosophical speculation. An invitation is not an information item to be catalogued with other knowledge of the world. An invitation requires a response. It is best characterized or understood in the totality of the event including both claim and response. Positive theology is not grounded in a special knowledge or information about the world; but it is grounded in the givenness of an event. The event is symbolic and gives rise to thought.

The word of forgiveness given to the followers of Jesus and ultimately to the world is a word of acceptance and a word of invitation. The hierophanous character of Jesus' proclamation is not found in the disclosure of new information about the architecture of the world or in propositions about the nature of ultimate reality. When the word of acceptance by God is heard, the possibility for seeing oneself as conditioned and limited vis-á-vis an unconditional and ultimate reality is manifested. The infinite distance separating the conditioned self from ultimate reality ceases to be experienced only as a judgment against the self. The reality of the contrast becomes in the context of acceptance also the possibility for the consciousness of a new future and a new being. The proclamation of forgiveness is a new predicate assigned by God to the relationship between man and God. The elementary definition of transcendence as a conjunction of actuality and possibility is applicable to the interpretation of this hierophany. The word of acceptance is the condition for a new posture toward the unlimited range of possibilities in the reality of God. The conjunction of these possibilities with the actuality of the human condition is the ontological foundtion for a new consciousness, a new being. The word of acceptance is hierophanous because it gives the possibility for a vision of the nearness of God. The word of God which was given to the disciples by Jesus is now the giver of a new consciousness. Positive theology depends on the fact that the given gives.

The givenness of a hierophanous *event* to the Christian community is clearly shown in the communities response to the death of Jesus. The kerygma of the earliest church is the proclamation of an event. Jesus, who was the bearer of the word of God, was drawn into the word of God as its essential content. "The proclaimer became the proclaimed."[12]

The appearance of the risen Christ bears witness that the word of God given in the proclamation of Jesus continues to give beyond the death of Jesus. The Christ-event is a manifestation of the power of the word of forgiveness within the continuing life of the Christian community. It is the Christ-event that is the primary symbol giving rise to positive theological reflection. It is the Christ-event that leads positive theology beyond foundational theology. The Christ-event is the historical visibility or sacramental presence of the word of God. Unlike foundational theology, dogmatic theology is marked by presence rather than by limits and absence. It is the presence of the word of God as an event that continues to give beyond the grave of Jesus. When the church continues to proclaim the word of God, the sacramental presence of the Christ-event continues to give the possibility for a new being.

The Christ-event is not equivalent to the Christmas story. The Christ-event was and remains a speaking and hearing of the word of God. Both the proclamation of Jesus and the proclamation about Jesus are proclamations of the word of forgiveness. The witness that Jesus died for our sins and that Christ is risen is an assurance of the early Christian community that the Christ-event is not a historical contingency but that it is the foundation for the consciousness of a new being. A positive theology born out of the witness of the Christ-event does not alter the topography of sacred markings with the addition of new artifacts, sacred placed or sacred times. Instead the word of forgiveness graspable in the sacrament of the Christ-event alters the consciousness of sacred markings so that they can be meaningfully integrated into the affirmation of life instead of standing as judgments against life. This is probably most clearly observed in the claim that there is a victory over death in the preaching of the resurrected Christ. Death is real, but Paul asks in Ist Corinthians, "O Death, where is your sting?" "The sting of death is sin" and the power of sin is abrogated in the word of forgiveness. Death has not been altered but the consciousness of death is radically different. Death is no longer a judgment against life. The power to move to the boundaries of human experience extends the effective range of live and gives a new meaning to self affirmation. The vision of transcendence is no longer a forbidden mystery.

The markings of transcendence which indicated the limits of secular consciousness and were a judgment upon its adequacy have been transformed through the word of forgiveness into the calling for a new consciousness of life. The Christ-event means the availability of transcendence or, if we prefer, the availability of God. As neo-orthodox theologians often reminded us, theology must proceed from the word of God to an understanding of reality and not from an understanding of the world to the word of God. This is the importance of a clear understanding of the distinction between the tasks of foundational and dogmatic theology. In dogmatic theology, God is graspable because of the word of acceptance. Transcendence moves from the boundary into the range of meaningful experience.

Hermeneutics which has come to be understood as the laying open of a text, a language or an experience which delivers a message has a special meaning when referred to the word of God. A hermeneutic of the word of God is not an interpretation of a sacred text or words attributed to God by some community. A hermeneutic of the word of God is the laying open of the world of experience by hearing the word of God. Hearing the word of God is an event which interprets life. The word of God is given to a community. The maintenance of this word gives rise to thought. It gives rise to interpretation. The word of God is fundamentally experienced in the life of a community as an act of interpretation. Thus, the search for divine *logia* independent from the word or event of forgiveness is a misunderstanding of the function of the word of God.

II

The concept of the word of God has been rightly equated with God's action by biblical scholars. Bultmann has said that the importance of the word of God is that it is spoken and not that it conveys eternal truth.[13] The concept of the word is bound to be a concept of the manifestation of power. Thus, it would be a mistake to assume that the word of God is identical with a biblical text. A text is an interpretation and a response to the word of God. This is why Barth suggests that we are to live with a text until it disappears and we can then confront the word of God.[14]

The word of God is not accessible as an object for scientific investigation since there is no text with which it can be identified. In fact the word of God is not itself accessible to phenomenological studies or a topography of sacred markings since it does not have objective characteristics. Only the event of hearing the word of God can be brought into the range of phenomenological inquiry. But, even this assertion can be misleading. Robert Funk notes that it was precisely the unavailability of an objective presentation of the word of God that led Ebeling and Fuchs to a remarkable and similar conclusion that the word of God is not interpreted by the exegete but that the word interprets.[15] This suggestion from historical and biblical scholarship is in basic agreement with our earlier statement that the word of God is fundamentally experienced as act of interpretation. This interpretation transforms a topography of sacred markings into a witness of the nearness of God.

This new hermeneutic recognizes that the theological task is not basically concerned with understanding the word of God, but it is concerned with the understanding of existence through the word of God. It is the word-event that illuminates existence. It is through hearing the word of acceptance that we can be free to see life in a context of ultimacy. The word of God mediates understanding. It lays open the fullness of experience.[16]

The inheritance of the word of God is the unconcealment of the possibility for dwelling in nearness with the stranger, with manifestations of ultimacy in nature, and with the meaning of the self. Thus, the landscape in a topography of sacred markings can become a familiar neighborhood filled with meanings that nourish individuation processes.

All of the above considerations view hearing of the word of God primarily as an event and not as a means to gain knowledge. "How is it possible to undergo an experience with language?" This is the transcendental question that lies behind the development of hermeneutical inquiry. This question is as fundamental for hermeneutical reflection as is the question concerning the possibility for objective knowledge for classical epistemology.

In the second chapter it is already shown that a developed conception of an experience with language or of the participation in a word-event is an essential characteristic of the sacramental interpretation of the word of God. We have in this chapter returned to the significance of the foundational theological question: "How does language function so that the resurrected Christ is visible to the disciples on the Emmaus road?" Now we may want to ask this question differently. "How does the word of God interpret experience so that the reality of the Christ is visible in the stranger?" The word of God as a hermeneutic calls for new reflection on the dialectical function of language and the multivalence of symbolism.

The multiplicity of language functions denies the possibility of univocal expression in the interpretation of the word of God or interpretation by the word of God. There is no question that one of the functions of language is to point toward its empirical reference. Language has an ostensive and descriptive function. However, because language contributes to the becoming of actual occasions it also has a carrying or ontological function. The structures of our being in the world are dynamic and formal. The objective appearance of the external world to consciousness has its foundations in formal structures. The ontological or event function of language is a dynamic consideration. It is the dialectical relationship between the realization of formal achievements in the content of understanding and the possibilities for creative passage in the act of understanding that constitute the full meaning of a word-event. The conception that the symbol gives rise to thought or that the word of God gives rise to theological reflection is a nascent conception of the ontological relationship between the content and the act of understanding. The restoration of meaning to a dynamic conception of the word-event in foundational theology is the restoration of the ontological significance of language functioning. The ontological importance of language functioning can be recognized even without the consideration of a specific content. But the actual character of dialectical passage into the future is always bound to the specific content of the word-event.

In itself, the relationship between language functioning and consciousness denotes a conjunction of actuality and possibility. Word as event is necessarily a transcendent act. This does not mean that the content of the word-event is a disclosure of transcendence. The act is transcendent and the content of the act participates in transcendence. The meaning of the word-event always overflows its content. Thus the restlessness that accompanies the incompleteness of language content has an ontological as well as psychological justification. The sense of reality that sanctions the meaning of language content is not always a judgment about the content of a word-event but is a response to the experience of a new connectedness determined by the conjunction of actuality with possibility in the dynamic realization of the word-event.

Since it is a naive oversimplification to identify our sense of reality with the content of objective understanding, it would be a mistake to talk about the reality of the word-event only in terms of the content of proclamation. The primary signification of the word *reality* still lies in our feelings of connectedness with the world. The ontological function of language alters this connectedness through the propositional conjunction of actuality and possibility. Language is intimately bound up with our sense or reality. In this sense all word-events are interpretive of experience. The word of God in the proclamation of the kerygma alters the quality of our connectedness with the world and thus transforms the reality of experience. The content of a proclamation of forgiveness gives rise to a new dialectic. The new reality is not identifiable with the message of forgiveness but it is bound up with the dialectical passage initiated by this proclamation. The word-event is both the content and the act of becoming which encompasses the hearing of the word of God. The shift from God, the judge, to God the accepting father is a fundamental alteration of our relationship to the world. Since the actualities of experience are defined by emergent processes of connectedness, not only is experience interpreted by the word-event in a simple sense of interpretation, but interpretation is a new connectedness, a new reality. The experiential manifestation of the conjunction of actuality and possibility in the word-event can be a new consciousness. This, however, is a secondary process in higher experience and is a function of variability and contrast. The transformation of reality in a word-event can remain below the threshold of consciousness and initiate a secret vocation. What this means is that the word-event can constitute a calling to a deeper involvement in life or to the boundaries of experience without the explicit statement of such a claim. This has important meaning for understanding the translation and proclamation of the word of God.

There are many reasons why we cannot speak *about* God. The obvious reason that God cannot be objectified without being limited has sometimes prematurely closed the discussion and has confused the meaning of speaking of God or proclaiming the word of God. The most important consideration in warning against speaking about God is that on the pretense of objective knowledge the inquirer can fail to recognize the ontological and sometimes unconscious significance of word-events. The dynamics of the act of knowing must be acknowledged as integral to understanding the word of God. The multivalence of religious language is grounded in the multiple functions of language. The word of God is symbolic because it participates in the becoming of reality.

When we talk specifically about the translation of the kerygma of the early church across history into the kerygma of the contemporary church, we are not talking about the alteration of content so that it is more palatable for modern taste. The kerygma is translated only when the word of proclamation has the same transforming power as did the understanding of the kerygma in the primitive church. This transforming power is a function of the word of God and constitutes the meaning of the word-event. The word of God has power when it is heard. The apologetic task of theology is to provide the conditions so that the word can be heard. It is the word-event and not prolegomena to the word-event that provides a new vision.

If the word of God were equated only with the *content* of Jesus' preaching or the preaching of the primitive Christian church, then we might think that the task of modern theology is to construct a fresh restatement of this content in a contemporary idiom. Theologians have often thought that their primary job was to offer an alternative expression of the "wisdom" of the gospel in the more precise language of Whitehead, the existential categories of Heidegger, or even through the secularized world-view of Sartre. In each case the foundational and dogmatic functions of theology are confused. The kerygma is properly understood only as a word-event. The kerygma is to be heard and it gives rise to positive dogmatic theology. This does not imply that the kerygma cannot be proclaimed to modern man in his own language if he has ears to hear. But the kerygma ceases to be kerygma if it is exclusively identified with the content of any message. If viewed only as the content of a new knowledge or as a new information item, the kerygma ceases to be important to modern man. As word-event or as hermeneutic, the kerygma is a matter of ultimate concern. Philosophy serves theology when it prepares the way for hearing the word of God. The content of philosophical achievement in foundational theology has a different language function than the proclamation of the word of God in preaching or dogmatic theology. Philosophy can carry us into new regions of experiencing; the word of forgiveness transforms our posture toward the world. The word of God cannot be substituted for philosophical reflection; philosphy cannot be substituted for the kerygma. Dogmatic theology is not a phenomenology of sacred markings.

III

The eschatological preaching of Jesus is a proper subject of dogmatic theology. The eschatological significance of the word of God does not preclude its existential significance. We must clarify this point since dogmatic theology articulates and interprets the eschatological meaning of the word of God. In its interpretations of eschatological meaning dogmatic theology should be informed by foundational theology about the multiple functions of language and the multivalence of symbols. The foundational interpretation of language usage bears upon the interpretation of the eschatological meaning of preaching the word of God.

There are two distinguishable meanings of eschatology related to the structural distinction between the act and content of a word-event. The content of the word of God in Israel's religion of expectation, in the teachings of Jesus, and in the expression of hope for the return of Christ is a content of promise. The promises of the coming of a yet unrealized reality and a yet unrealized fulfillment give eschatological content to the word of God in the Judeo-Christian tradition. This dimension of the eschatological significance of the word of God, so well articulated by Jürgen Moltmann, is correlated with but distinguishable from the existential meaning of the act of speaking and hearing the word of God. Moltmann's dictum that "hope alone is to be called 'realistic' because it alone takes seriously the possibilities with which all reality is fraught" is applicable beyond his study of the content of the word of God.[17] The contrasting content of promise is conjoined with descriptions of actuality for the experience of a vivid presence. This contrast of the actual and the possible is the ontological foundation for a new consciousness. The new consciousness born in the hearing of the word of God is not bound to the contingencies of historical circumstance. Hearing the word of God transcends the immediacy of historical limitations. The word-event is beyond the determinations of history. That is, the word-event is an eschatological act because its meanings and determination extend beyond and are not bound by its inherited historical circumstances.

Since a positive theology of the word of God is to be understood in the dialectical context of content and act, the eschatological meanings of both dimensions of the word-event belong to a mature assessment of the possibilities for contemporary theology. The seemingly contradictory relationships to historical consciousness in the investigation of these two aspects of the word-event have too long obscured the importance of their dialectical relationship. We must understand the meaning of the claim that the word of God is simultaneously in time and not subject to time. It is my suggestion that the recognition of the existential meaning of eschatological preaching by Bultmann and the rediscovery of the historical promise of eschatological preaching by Moltmann can be reconciled in the understanding of the multiple functions of word usage.

Moltmann characterizes the diverse emphases on the revelatory disclosures of the subjectivity of God or of authentic selfhood as hallmarks of epiphany religions. The gods of the epiphanies are then contrasted with the God of promise.[18] The epiphany religions are concerned with the unveiling of the eternal which breaks the bondage of time rather than with an eschatological hope that waits for the realization of realities that are not yet a part of historical experience. He is afraid that theological construction has sometimes transformed the Judeo-Christian religion of promise into a religion of the epiphanies. Does this description apply to our understanding of the word-event? Does the focus on the presence of the eternal distort and render meaningless the promise of the future? It could be charged that the development of transcendental eschatology is actually a return to archaic ontological conceptions in which reality is a function of archetypal structures.[19] Here, eschatology is the overcoming of time. The revelation of archetypal structures is equivalent to the revelation of the possibility for authentic self realization. Hence, these structures are transcendental. Transcendental eschatology appears to have a closer relationship to a remembrance of origins than to a promise of the future.

It must be admitted that if we only examine the content of the eschatological word of God, it is correct to say that the promises of the Christian gospel do not remove us from history or abrogate the limitations of time. The message of Jesus is that we are at the beginning of a new aeon. This message is delivered in historical categories. Christianity is a religion of expectation that waits and looks for the coming of Christ.[20] Theology should sharpen the expectations and hopes of the waiting Christian community and surrender its interest and pretensions concerning absolute knowlege. This suggests that trust in the promise of future realization delays talk of the essential self and the knowledge of a God who is the beginning and the end, Alpha and Omega. The content of promise leaves the conception of eternity in a shroud of mystery.

This characteristic of a religion of expectation is recognized by Moltmann but strangely enough it is not viewed as problematic. He says that a person who trusts himself to a revelation of promise is a riddle unto himself. This person views himself as a *homo absconditus.*[21]

The proclamation of promise does not bring the individual home to an eternal reality to which many persons have felt that they belong and from which they were estranged by the limitations of temporal passage. The promise does not satisfy the unrestricted desire to know. Images of the horizon of promise are historical instead of ontological. Life is reoriented toward the future in Moltmann's historical rendering of a theology of hope. Immediate experience is no longer the primary datum for the adjudication of reality. In fact, Moltmann says that the word of promise has not found a realty congruous with it. The word of promise stands in contradiction to the reality which is now open to our experience. To him, this is the implication of the conception of promise.[22]

Moltmann's admission that the man of promise is *homo absconditus* and that there is no reality open to our experience that is congruous with the reality of the promise seriously calls into question the meaning and the credibility of the content of the promise. The content of promise seems meaningless to modern man because the search for immediate referents to the language of the promise is denied by Moltmann's conception of promise. Directly related to the problem of meaning and the vacuum of experience associated with the religion of promise is the problem of credibility. Why should anyone believe a promise for which there is no experience that witnesses to its significance. The fruit of the promise in our everyday lives according to this interpretation is that the possibilities for essential selfhood remain hidden from the actual self. The content of a promise does not justify itself. We consider most visions of a utopian future as naive. Why can we take seriously the promise of the Christian gospel? Severing the dialectic between the content and act of a word-event through the strong polemic against transcendental eschatologies leaves Moltmann's position without a meaningful ground. Without the concept of a dialectic between act and content of language usage, the possibilities of the promise are possibilities that belong to the future and not to the present. The appearance of the promise is not considered a disclosure of possibilities. The appearance of the promise is not conceived as an epiphany that validates the promise. Moltmann says that the point of the appearance is the promise and that the promise directs our attention away from the appearance or epiphany. Moltmann does not consider the revelation of the promise a hierophanous event. It is the content of the promise that is of religious significance to him and this content points to a hierophany that is yet outstanding in history.[23] Because the possibilities of the promise belong to the future and not to the appearance of the promise we cannot understand the promise as a transcendent act. Because the possibilities are not available or usable in the passage through experience they would not be viewed as constitutive of the reality of the present situation. It is with this view that we have taken issue. It does clarify the importance of the content if we directly address the theology of hope with the question, "What gives credibility to the content of the promise of the word of God". Moltmann addresses himself to this question without turning to foundational theology.

There are two senses in which the historical nature of the content of the promise of the word of God are given credibility without dissolving the future of the promise in subjectivist irrelevancies. The truth of promises to Israel are recognized in partial fulfillment in the history of Israel. Or we may say that the God of promise can be recognized in the history of Israel. Moltmann says that there is an overspill to these promises and that the recognition of fulfillment is not identical with the full realization of the promises of God. "Every reality in which a fulfillment is already taking place now, becomes the confirmation, exposition and liberation of a greater hope."[22] Promises enter the process of fulfillment but they are not completely realized in any historical event. The overspill of promise points to the possibilities that belong to the future. But, the recognition of the God of promise in history confirms and strengthens the hope of the believer in the promise.

The fundamental datum for Christian eschatology is the resurrection and future of Christ.[25] More important than the recognition of the God of promise in the history of Israel is the proleptic nature of the resurrection appearances of the Christ. The appearances of the resurrected Christ anticipate the meaning of the future in the coming glory of God. The Christ-event is a paradigm governing the meaning of the eschatological future. In the incarnation the future of God is given historical visibility. The resurrection is the place where eschatology intersects history.[26] The resurrection appearances of the crucified Christ give a preview of the coming glory of God that anchors the Christian consciousness which waits and hopes. The resurrection discloses possibilities that are a possession of the future. Because these possibilities are a property of the future and not the present they are bound to the experience of hope instead of self realization. The "reality-prolepsis" of the Easter story aims not at an existential reinterpretation of the human situation but at Christian mission. Whatever Moltmann sees in this Christian mission that calls us forth does not include the existential verification or mediation of the Christ-event. The man of hope remains *homo absconditus*. This means that his hope and his mission rooted in the "reality-prolepsis" of the resurrection appearances depends upon the historical witness of the early church.

Thus, the biblical witness to the resurrection is here viewed as the foundation of Christian hope. Our knowledge of the God of the future manifested in the Christ-event is not a direct part of our experience. It is the experience of the early church. Because God is of the future and witness to the Christ-event belongs to the past, we live in the interval between promise and fulfillment. Since the future is not yet, we are dependent upon the witness of the past. If the credibility of the apostolic witness is threatened we are in danger of being disinherited from the force of the promise. Gilkey raises the obvious question in his critique of Moltmann, "Why should we believe these reports?"[27] There is much in the New Testament that we do not accept. Without existential verification, what is compelling about the apostolic witness to the incredible resurrection appearances? Without the judgment of immediate experience, how can we be sure that the promise of the coming glory of God is not accepted only because it gives us comfort as a wishful projection?

The disconnectedness of the theology of hope from the court of experiential decision is vividly portrayed against the background of recent Jewish suffering. The recognition of the God of promise in the history of Israel introduces problems into a theology of hope that are not easily overcome by the "reality-prolepsis" in the resurrection of Christ. Theologically bound to a conception of the fulfillment of promise in the history of Israel is the conception of punishment or divine retribution. The Old Testament theology that recognizes Israel's God of promise has also interpreted every catastrophe in Israel's history as the punishment of an unfaithful people. The implications of this type of theology are that Auschwitz and Buchenwald are implementations of God's promise. In its most hideous expression, a Christian theology of hope could be led to interpret the holocaust as a manifestation of the cross in the "reality-prolepsis" of the Easter story. Even without such an added interpretation the historical reality of the holocaust calls into question the waiting for the coming glory of God. Richard Rubenstein thinks that the implications of the traditional theology of history are too obscene to accept.[28] How can we believe in a God of the promise "after Auschwitz?"

In the experience of many contemporary men the holocaust is a forceful prolepsis of the future. It overshadows the Easter story. In the words of holocaust survivor Elie Wiesel, "I belong to a generation sensitized to the extreme, trained to attach more significance to threats than to promises."[29] Can a God of promise that does not manifest himself in the immediacy of experience give hope to a people that have been sensitized to the extreme? The manifestations of radical evil are part of the reality that belongs to the present. The gods of evil have not withdrawn from our sight. The despair of a theology of hope that recognizes only the Christ who was historically visible in the past and has power over the future is that the present belongs to the manifestations of radical evil. For many men the threat of evil overshadows the credibility of the promise of the not yet realized glory of God. A theology of hope cannot live by the *content* of the promise alone.

The hermeneutic of the word of God is greatly expanded in a dialectical conception of a word-event. There is no sense in which the force of the content of the word-event or promise is abrogated by examination of the act of a word-event. In fact, an understanding of the dialectic between act and content frees the content to manifest itself in its own terms. The content of the promise can be fully future oriented while the act of hearing the word of God has its ontological status in the present situation. To even talk about hearing the word of God as a word-event is to acknowledge the importance of the act. It is the act that is transcendent, and it is the act that gives existential meaning to the words of promise.

The realism of hope is founded in a posture that takes seriously the realm of possibilities. The promise of the word of God is future oriented but this future is articulated in the language of past and present experience. Even though Moltmann insists that the promise is fulfilled only in the future, the words of promise are drawn from recognizable realities. The return to the land, the generation of a people, or the kingdom of God are images that are not congruent with actualities in modern experience. But, the imagery of promise conjoins possibilities with the actuality of experience. As an ontological qualifier the word of promise is the articulation of possibilities.

The conjunction of these possibilities with the actuality of experience establishes the necessary contrast for a new consciousness. This new consciousness has existential immediacy and gives credibility to the content of the promise. The new consciousness born out of the eschatological articulation of possibility has a hierophanous character. The world is viewed differently. Our eyes can be opened to the realities of life because the conjunction of possibility with actuality provides the contrast to ontologically ground conscious disclosure of a new world. The intensity of the new consciousness is proportionate to the severity of the contrast and the significance of the conjunction between actuality and the realm of possibilities. The new consciousness is not a new perspective that can be attributed to a geographical change or its equivalent. The new consciousness is an ontological change explained by the propositional structure of ontological passage in higher phases of experience.[30]

The historical reference of the content of promise is in the future and the ontological reference of the act of promise is in the present. There is an immediacy to the word of God and the word of God has power over the future. The word of promise is instrumental in the birth of the new consciousness and the new consciousness then bears an existential witness to the credibility of the promise. The promise points beyond itself.

In conclusion we can say that the eschatological significance of the word of God is inextricably bound to the existential significance of the word of God. The theology of hope has its foundation in the dialectic between the act and content of the word of God. The hermeneutic of the word of God authenticates the promise that carries us into the future.

Notes

1. Karl Jaspers, *Philosophical Faith and Revelation* (New York: Harper and Row, 1967), p. 94.
2. *Ibid.*, p. 100.
3. Karl Rahner, *Hearers of the Word* (New York: Herder and Herder, 1969), p. 168.
4. Paul Tillich, *Systematic Theology,* 3 Vols. (Chicago: University of Chicago Press, 1951, 1957, 1963) III, pp. 223, 224.
5. Paul Ricoeur, *The Symbolism of Evil* (New York: Harper and Row, 1967), p. 348.
6. See Rudolf Bultmann, *Jesus and the Word* (New York: Charles Scribner's Sons, 1934), p. 30.
7. Gerhard Ebeling, *The Nature of Faith* (Philadelphia: Fortress Press, 1967), p. 183.
8. Bultmann, p. 39, 151.
9. Cf. Joachim Jeremias, *New Testament Theology* (New York: Charles Scribner's Sons, 1971), p. 85.
10. Bultmann, p. 219.
11. Jeremias, p. 113.
12. Rudolf Bultmann, *Theology of the New Testament,* 2 Vols. (New York: Charles Scribner's Sons, 1951, 1955), I, p. 33.
13. Rudolf Bultmann, *Faith and Understanding,* I (New York: Harper and Row, 1969), p. 287.
14. Robert W. Funk, *Language, Hermeneutic and Word of God* (New York: Harper and Row, 1966), p. 11.
15. *Ibid.*, p. 11.
16. See Gerhard Ebeling, *Word and Faith* (Philadelphia: Fortress Press, 1963) Chapter XI for a development of the concept that the word of God has a hermeneutic function.
17. Jürgen Moltmann, *Theology of Hope* (New York: Harper and Row, 1967), p. 25.
18. *Ibid.*, pp. 42-45.
19. See Mircea Eliade, *Cosmos and History* (New York: Harper Torchbooks, 1959), p. 39 for clarification of this conception.
20. Moltmann, p. 31. Moltmann reminds us that in the practical wisdom of the church it is the coming of Christ and not his eternal presence that is celebrated in Advent hymns.
21. *Ibid.*, p. 91.
22. *Ibid.*, p. 103.
23. *Ibid.*, p. 100.
24. *Ibid.*, pp. 106-109.
25. *Ibid.*, p. 195.
26. Carl E. Braaten, *Christ and Counter-Christ* (Philadelphia: Fortress Press, 1972), p. 50.
27. Jürgen Moltmann and Frederick Herzog, ed., *The Future of Hope* (New York: Herder and Herder, 1970), p. 87.
28. Richard Rubenstein, *After Auschwitz* (Indianapolis: Bobbs-Merrill, 1966), p. 153.
29. Elie Wiesel, *One Generation After* (New York: Avon Books, 1972), p. 175.
30. See Chapter 4.

CHAPTER VIII

THE PROCLAMATION
OF THE
WORD OF GOD

𝒯he primary function and mission of the Christian church is the proclamation of the word of God. The fullness of Christian life can be understood only in relation to the meaning of the word-event. The hermeneutic of the word of God is the necessary foundation for unmasking the institutional church and revealing the communion of possibility.

The definition of ministry is on the deepest level also grounded in the meaning of the word-event. Thus a practical theology which investigates the ministry of proclamation must also be derived from the hermeneutic of the word of God. A ministry of proclamation and the church which is the communion of possibility are essentially related.

A mature conception of the ministry unfettered from social conventions and the complacency of institutional requirements can be discovered only through responsiveness to the interpretive power of the word-event. The familiar willingness of the institutional church to compromise with social success and view its ministers as the guardians of relative social values has unwittingly separated the everyday life of the church from the eschatological realities of the kingdom of God. The role of ministry in separation from the proclamation of the word of God is dictated by the most powerful or articulate voices in the society. In this distorted view, society decides how the minister can best serve its needs which are determined by its own secular analysis. When it is expedient the minister is trained in a secular science and licensed by governmental or secular accrediting agencies. Then the minister can be expected to serve societal needs as they have been determined by secular understanding. Certainly this ministry can be important and fruitful but it is not a ministry of proclamation. Christian ministry can be resident in the parish, in the marketplace, or in secular institutions, but its identity and power come first from the hermeneutic of the word of God.

The ministry that is rooted in the word-event interprets the realities of the situation to which it is addressed. It is the interpretation of a situation by the word of God that defines the needs of a people to which a Christian ministry can powerfully respond. James Dittes illustrates this point in relationship to the first account of a healing ministry in the *Acts of the Apostles*.[1] When a lame man saw Peter and John on their way into the temple at the ''Beautiful Gate'' he asked for charity. Instead of allowing the man to define his needs and the character of their ministry, they interpreted his needs through the word of God and offered him healing. Their ministry was determined by the consciousness of possibility rooted in the interpretive power of God's word. Their healing ministry was actually a ministry of proclamation. The perception of need was adjusted to the eschatological realities of the word-event. We can say that healing ministry is the hermeneutic of the word of God. Peter addressed those who gathered around him in astonishment by saying ''the name of Jesus, by awakening faith, has strengthened this man . . . this faith has made him completely well.'' (Acts 3:16) The transformation of the remoteness of God into the nearness of God in the word of acceptance discloses new possibilities that ontologically conjoin with actuality and carry us into a new future. The hermeneutic of the word of God is a revelation of possibility which can be translated into a ministry of healing.

The distinguishing mark of a ministry of proclamation is its eschatological significance. The disclosure of new possibilities allows the minister to respond to people more seriously than they respond to themselves. This is what Karl Barth meant when he said that the situation on Sunday morning is an eschatological situation.[2] The desire for an ultimate event is realistic because the word-event is an eschatological reality. The meaningful absence of dimensions of ultimacy in secular understanding can be transformed into a meaningful presence when the proclamation of the word gives rise to thought. When the interpretive disclosure of possibilities is conjoined with the actuality of a situation, a new consciousness is born which transcends the situation. Even the dawning of this new consciousness brings us into the fellowship of the eschatological community of the kingdom of God. The new consciousness of reality judges the adequacy of old levels of expectation and carries us into the future.

I

Understanding the dialectic between the act and content of speaking and hearing is the transcendental foundation for a reassessment of the ministry of proclamation. A ministry of the word cannot be evaluated by judging the orthodoxy of the content of proclamation. The word-event is act as well as content and functions ontologically in the dynamics of creative passage. The "truth" of the Christian faith is a characteristic of involvement that modifies the ontological or "carrying" function of language. The ostensive and descriptive functions of the content of language have their truth value dialectically subsumed under the significance of the precipitated act of understanding. The failure of preaching is often the failure to allow the word to become event by artifically circumscribing the relationship to the actual circumstances of the situation that a dialectical movement will naturally transcend. This is sometimes evident in the community's exaggerated concern for harmony or acceptable decorum. The relevance and meaning of the word-event should be experienced with reference to the newly emergent consciousness and not with reference to old levels of expectation. The ministry of proclamation cannot be conformed to old expectations because it is a disclosure of a new relationship to the world.

The dialectical achievement of a new consciousness in the word-event is a dimension of Christian freedom that has been long recognized in tradition. Paul addressed the Romans by saying "Do not be conformed to this eon, but be transformed by the renewal of your mind." (Romans 12:2) The danger of a weak ministry is that it conforms the proclamation of the word of God to the expectations of society. The content of preaching is viewed as information instead of being viewed as address and invitation. Dialectical movement depends upon the conjunction and contrast of actuality and possibility.

Because the word of God is a word of acceptance or forgiveness it must have an object. Forgiveness is an act that has meaning only when it is related to a concrete situation. The word of acceptance alters a relationship and has the particularity of a real situation.

Efforts have been made to deny language its many voices. For example, viewing the *kerygma* as objective history conforms proclamation to secular expectations that only recognize the descriptive meaning of language. The descriptive function of language points but it does not invite. Of course, language is in fact always symbolic and multivalent because it has an ontological function. But this multiplicity of language functions can be hidden by anticipations of meaning that are one dimensional. Thus, the stupor of conformity truncates the fullness of the word-event. Any estrangement from consciousness of the ontological function of language is felt as a loss of power and meaning.

For example, the exclusive concern with the content of the word-event imbues theology and preaching with a false sense of objectivity. The consequent probing of the content of proclamation with an "Enlightenment" commitment is disinterested and neutral objectivity becomes a forgetfulness of language functions. The ideal of objectivity confines proclamation within an artificial perimeter so that it is an object or experience beside other objects or experiences in the world. In this context the word of God exists for its own sake. The word of God is no longer the power of revelation among other revelations. The strangeness of this view of revelation is that the word of God says so little about reality. When the content of proclamation is viewed in isolation from the fullness of the word-event, it may be interesting but it is not a matter of ultimate concern. There is experienced a loss of meaning for the separation of the content from the act of proclamation is in fact an isolation of the content from realities of the world around us. The vitality of the word has been misplaced.

When the existential function of language is lost the foundation of proclamation is thought to be the exposition of a sacred text. The content of the text becomes the object of understanding. Understanding the text in itself and by itself is the hallmark of a distorted ministry of the word. It is easy to explain why this conception of the word of God restricts the minister to the pulpit. If his task is to interpret the text, then he must organize his ministry around the study of the text. The sermon is the obvious vehicle for a ministry that is exclusively concerned with the content of the word of God. This one dimensional conception of the word of God is the foundation of a one dimensional conception of the ministry. The Bible loses its voice and becomes a sacred object. Christian ministry can become dangerously confused with Christian piety.

In contrast, the hermeneutic of the word of God is a multidimensional conception which expands the meaning of ministry. In a dialectical understanding of language usage, the content of language is never there only for its own sake. The meaning of the content is founded in the act of proclamation. The proclamation of a text has its full significance only when it is conceived of as a word-event. It is the word-event that is the origin, meaning, and future of a text.[3] In this conception it is the word that interprets existence. The word directs ministry out of the sanctuary into the world which it interprets.

When proclamation is directed into the world it is given the concreteness of feelings. The dialectical conception of the word is empty without historical embodiment in actual occasions. The importance of historical embodiment emphasizes the sacramental quality of the word-event. The world witnesses to the nearness of God if our consciousness is transformed by the word-event. Ministry recovers its living sacramental base because the act of proclamation is directed toward the everydayness of experience The actuality of the world of feeling is brought into consciousness by its conjunction and contrast with possibility. Thus, the proclamation of the word of God to the world is both judgment, the call to repentence, and grace, the realization of meaning.

The available realities of everyday experience witness to the nearness of God when viewed with a new consciousness. For example, bread and wine have a sacramental meaning in the fellowship of a new consciousness. Table fellowship becomes the celebration of new feelings and new meanings.

We have now recognized that the content of proclamation does not itself explain the disclosure of new feelings that are associated with the sacramental valorization of the world. But foundational theology contributes to our analysis the notion from the general theory of language functioning that conceptual content is transcended by the fullness of action. Thus, the content of proclamation is transcended by the fullness of the word-event. The fullness of the word-event includes the passage into a new actuality. The new relationships or the new feelings that constitute this emergent occasion reach beyond the content of the word in a conjunction with the ontological inheritance of a past concreteness. A new consciousness is the privileged state of a newly emergent occasion but it should be noted that this consciousness does not exhaust the meaning of the occasion. There are not yet conscious relationships that are part of the fullness of ontological action in the sacramental valorization of the world. The new consciousness is only the privileged manifestation of the new being.

We noted in the philosophical interpretation of hermeneutics that consciousness participates in its own foundation through the use of language. The foundation of consciousness exceeds conscious manifestations in the formation of new relationships This means that the word-event has more significance than is indicated in conscious experience. The word-event contributes to the complexity of satisfaction in the ontological passage toward a new concreteness. The grant of language is experienced as the gift of a new consciousness, but more importantly, the grant of language is the gift of a new being signified by the new consciousness. That there can be a new consciousness indicates that there can be a new concreteness. The proclamation of the word of God is taken through consciousness into formative ontological processes that can then be marked by a new consciousness. The consequence of these processes is that the fullness of the word-event transcends the content of proclamation and even transcends the new consciousness emergent from the word-event.

This means that a ministry of proclamation goes beyond a conceptualization of the word of God. The power of the ministry of the word is experienced as a feeling of a new reality. The overspill of action beyond the limits of the content of the word adds a new dimension of meaning to the world of experience that even extends beyond the conceptual achievements of the newly formed consciousness of the world.

The stepping beyond the content of the word in the act of proclamation can be described as reason in ecstasy. Ecstasy is an appropriate description of the felt significance of the act of proclamation transcending the content of proclamation. When the ministry of the word realizes itself in the fullness of action, the experience of the community goes beyond its everydayness. The community becomes an ecstatic communion that witnesses to the power of the word. The ecstatic communion has hopes, dreams, and visions of possibilities that go beyond itself. It feels these realities toward which it is becoming.

II

The particularity of the word-event is a historical condition. The word is directed toward the world and is given a historical embodiment. The vision of an ecstatic communion is eschatological but it is not ahistorical. The revelatory significance of a ministry of proclamation is that the word of God transforms a topography of sacred markings into a witness of the nearness of God. A ministry of the word appears multidimensional because it addresses itself to a pluralistic world. The specializations of ministry are actually functions of its historical embodiment. However, the vocation of Christian ministry remains singular. Christian ministry is the proclamation of the word of God. Therefore, the unity of the call to ministry has many expressions because the word-event interprets the multiplicity of situations to which it is addressed. This exposition-event illuminates reality and, through the dialectical structure of language acts, transforms reality into a sacramental witness to the nearness of God. That is, the word of acceptance alters our relationship to the world so that new possibilities are manifested concerning our participation in reality. Through theological articulation those possibilities are conjoined with the actuality of our situation. The word that gives rise to theological reflection initiates a transformation of reality. The theological conjunction of possibility and actuality is an ontological foundation for passage into a new reality.

The ministry of proclamation can be viewed as a saving ministry and still maintain its sacramental quality. There is a threefold nature to this conception of salvation.[4] First, the word of acceptance is an act of justification. The immediate consequence of the Christ-event is that we are addressed by the presence of God "in spite of" the brokenness of our historical condition. Second, the word of acceptance allows us to see and participate in possibilities for a new reality. Third, the conjunction of these possibilities with the actuality of the historical situation dialectically transforms the reality of situation into a new concreteness.

The historical coloring and concrete expression of a saving ministry can be gleaned from the topography of sacred markings. That is, the topography of sacred markings opens up the hermeneutical circle so that the word can be heard. The proclamation of the word is particularized by the location of the hearer. The topography of sacred markings suggests that not all situations are equally amenable to the proclamation of the word and that not all people have ears to hear.

Through the ministry of the word of God, God becomes meaningfully present within a topography of sacred markings. The presence of the word is not itself a sacred marking. Hearing the word of God interprets the topography of sacred markings so that dimensions of ultimacy are felt inside of the boundaries of experience. Ministry of the word mediates understanding of the world so that sacred markings are not judgments against the poverty of experience, but they are manifestations of the possibility for a more abundant life. The ministry of the word interprets and apprehends the realities of the sacred revealed in our personal and collective biographies.

The dialectical conception of the ministry recognizes the primacy of action in the word-event. The illumination of sacred markings is not merely a conceptual notion. Meaning is a function of feelings or relationships and is only catalogued by abstractions. The ministry of the word is an involvement with the world and there is a discernment of meaning which arises from this involvement. The word of acceptance endows us with the power to accept the realities manifested in a topography of sacred markings. Since the apprehension of sacred markings is not necessarily a conceptual achievement, the acceptance of realities manifested in a topography of sacred markings may be an acceptance of feelings rather than ideas.

A ministry of the word is exciting because it is a reclamation of experience. The absence of meaning was painfully noticable on the boundaries of life. The word of acceptance allows man to approach the boundaries of experience and again grasp the possibilities for satisfaction in his state of becoming The dialectic of the word-event gives us both an immediate existential satisfaction and the hope for future fulfillment. The existential immediacy of the word-event assures us that meaning is present to experience and encourages us to reach for experience. A ministry of proclamation frees us to invest our lives in the daily world rather than renounce the world because it is empty of meaning. Proclamation gives situational presence to the interpretive power of the word of God. Ministry is the implementation of the interpretive power of the word of God.

III

Our elementary definition of religion was simply the human response to moments of transcendence. The ministry of proclamation qualifies those moments of transcendence with the interpretive power of the word of God. The topography of sacred markings demonstrated that there is a complicity of transcendence with secular life. This means that effective ministry must also integrate itself with secular life. There is no sense in which the word of God stands alone in an isolated sanctuary.

In earlier chapters on the topography of sacred markings we developed a map to help us locate manifestations of transcendence in secular life. This map can now illustratively serve us in suggesting practical regions of service for an effective ministry. Of course, the topography was only a methodological tool for focusing on some regions of experience that lie outside of the meaningful range of secular models of understanding. Thus, it can only be an exemplary tool contributing to the examination of forms for a practical definition of the ministry. The actual possibilities for the realization of a ministry of proclamation are as extensive as the full range of experience. The seven regions of experiencing indicated in the topography of sacred markings are only indicative of an immediate challenge to a contemporary ministry.

There was never a clear separation between comic, ludic, poetic, cosmic, dramatic, oneiric and neurotic dimensions of experiencing. They are characteristic expressions of a secular voice that is dissatisfied with the incompleteness of experience. They express the need for a reinterpretation of life. This muffled but articulate voice calls the minister back into the world.

Our first need is to be able to approach and enter these regions of experiencing with our eyes open. That is, the word of acceptance gives us the courage to participate in realities that call into question the adequacy of our lives as well as enrich our lives with new possibilities. The anxiety of judgment is overcome by the power of acceptance.

We have said that one characteristic of the topography of sacred markings was that dimensions of ultimacy were as meaningfully absent as they were present. The incompleteness of the experience is its most salient feature. The incompleteness of the experience is felt as a judgment upon the adequacy of the experience. This is why these regions of experiencing are not comfortable homes for secular man to find rest. Their excitement draws and repels at the same time.

For example, the essence of the comic is discrepancy, incongruity and incommensurability. It was noted sex and death play a significant role in the comic experience because they unmask conscious pretentions about the dignity of the individual. The comic experience is a recognition that we are not masters of our destiny. Comedy is an elementary expression of our finitude and a recognition of realities that shape our lives but extend beyond conscious control. A ministry of proclamation addresses the comic dimension of experience by addressing the realities that transcend our control and generate the comic situation. Such a ministry does not dissolve the significance of the comic experience but it allows the meaning of the comic experience to come to a full expression.

The comic dimension of life is real and is with us throughout our lives. Withdrawal from the comic is an attempt to withdraw from the reality and threat of our finitude. But the nature of the comic experience is that it destroys fantasized views of personal power and dignity. Without the power to accept the comic dimension of life as an expression of finitude, the comic experience appears as a threat to life. Humor darkens and the comic perspective on life becomes indistinguishable from a cynical perspective on life. The comic experience is not a threat to the ministry of proclamation because the word of God is accepting of our finitude. In fact, the ministry of acceptance turns the comic experience away from cynical resignation toward a celebration of the meanings that encompass us. Active ministry should deepen the significance of the comic dimension of life.

All of the regions of experiencing that were noted in the topography of sacred markings are suggestive of possibilities for the practical formulation of ministry. Even the recognition that man is *homo ludens* is related to a growing understanding of ministerial possibilities.[5] The church must be a community that is not bound by the exigencies of the moment. The ministry of the word unlocks dimensions of timelessness that are felt in the ludic experience. The liturgy of modern worship can then become profoundly self conscious of man as *homo ludens*. The rupturing of the wheel of time gives us a new perspective on the quality of everyday life. The freedom and festivity of play can imaginatively portray and intensify the intimations of joy that belong to experience.

The word of acceptance frees us from an ethic that is rooted in a doctrine of justification by works. A work ethic would question the meaningfulness of play because it detracts us from the business of salvation. In contrast, the word of acceptance lets play be play. It allows us to approach this often hidden sacred marking on the landscape of experience.

It becomes clearer that the significance of a ministry of proclamation rests with the interpretive power of the word of God that discloses dimensions of ultimacy and makes them approachable The whole range of experience is transformed by the illumination of ultimate meanings. Because the ultimate is not a function of lesser realities, the lesser realities are valued in terms of their own meanings.[6] The ministry of proclamation does not subordinate every experience to the service of salvation but unveils the reality of God in the presence of normal living. Life is allowed to proceed precisely because we are accepted through the grace of God. Play is a sacred marking because it ruptures the bondage of time. This is not the expressed purpose of play. In fact, Bonhoeffer is correct when he says that play is essentially removed from all subordination to purpose.[7] This is why to play is free from time and this is why we must be freed to participate in play. When the word of God interprets life so that we are free to play, play interprets experience so that we can feel the significance and joy of liberation from the bondage of time.

Throughout the full range of experience the ministry of proclamation discloses possibilities for a more profound grasp on the meanings of experience. The word of acceptance gives us the courage to risk a deeper involvement with life. We can begin to tell a story that places our lives in a context of ultimacy even though the dimension of ultimacy is a judgment upon our lives. The word of acceptance allows us to integrate our personal biographies with realities that go beyond our control but bear upon the definition of our lives. The poetic, oneiric, and cosmic dimensions of experiencing are manifestations of ultimate meanings in the dramatic rendering of experience. The ministry of the word comes to a mature realization when it grasps the depths of these experiences and helps us tell the story of our lives. The ministry of acceptance alters our relationship to experience so that we are not afraid to tell our story and it grants us an inheritance of symbols so that we have a language through which we can tell our story.

In the topography of sacred markings it was noted that the poetic, oneiric and cosmic dimensions of experiencing are not readily available in a secular culture. The word of acceptance prepares us to live in a fellowship that has the strength to confront the realities that are made known through a full participation in the poetic, oneiric and cosmic dimensions of life.

The strangeness of the poetic functioning of language in modern culture is its self conscious affinity with the ontological function of language. The poetic use of language unveils possibilities that ontologically conjoin with actuality to carry us into a new consciousness and a new concreteness. When the poet becomes forgetful of the ontological function of language, poetry becomes trite. The ministry of proclamation calls the poet to his true vocation and listens to his disclosure of possibility. The alliance of the minister and poet is an acknowledgment of the dialectical function of language and a commitment to the disclosure of possibilities that have become hidden through the forgetfulness of language in the busy commerce of everyday life. The communion of possibility needs the vision of the poet and the poet needs a community in which he can be heard. The resistance to the poetic disclosure of possibilities is rooted in the perversity of the intellect and not in its fallibility. The power of a ministry of proclamation is that it disarms the sting of finitude but allows for its manifestation. The communion of possibility is willing to be unmasked by the vision of the poet. It is willing to surrender the pretensions of a false mastery and dignity in order to honestly experience its home in a context of ultimacy. Thus, the ministry of the word sanctions the poetic recovery of language.

In all of the examples that have been cited it appears that Christian ministry prepares the community to meaningfully participate in the dynamics of a creative life. Christian life is directly contrasted with a neurotic pattern of experience which retreats from the exigencies of psychic life. The willingness to risk a full participation in experience without retreating from the limits of familiarity deepens our relationships with the graceful moments in our personal lives that nourish individuation processes and enrich our lives with new meanings

The ministry of acceptance is accepting of the whole person. That means that the grant of meaning that is buried in the unconscious and dramatically announces itself in oneiric symbols is also within the scope of pastoral ministry. The numinosity of the dream experience makes a direct claim on the understanding of the religious personality. Retreat from the shadowed symbols of individuation is not permissable when we proclaim a word of acceptance. A practical definition of ministry includes the inescapable alliance with a psychology of individuation. Thus, the communion of possibility must provide the occasion for the analysis of meanings that are announced by the unconscious in the lives of its participants. As was indicated in the topography, these symbols have collective as well as personal significance for the individuation process. This added complexity for practical ministry is just one of the implications of understanding the word of God as an invitation to a fuller life instead of as the revelation of a blueprint for life. It would be a very shallow concept of God's grace that would extricate man from the exigencies of psychic life in the fulfillment of selfhood. Unconscious demands are just as critical after hearing the word of God as before hearing the word of God. The difference is in the nature of our stance in the face of these realities. The communion of possibility says yes to the presence of these realities and includes them within the scope of the healing and interpretive power of the word of God.

The cosmic dimension of experiencing elaborates the need to integrate our personal story into a context of ultimate significance. The unrestricted desire to know extends inquiry beyond our immediate neighborhood in the search for meaning. We need a cosmic language to thematize our belonging to the world. This cosmic language may be a mythic-poetic language or it may be a metaphysical language. The need for the articulation of our place in the cosmos is a natural extension of the dramatic rendering of experience. Whether the functional need for cosmic expression is met by the revalorization of an earlier cosmogonic myth or by the construction of a new metaphysical myth, contemporary ministry must recognize that modern man is not at home in the cosmos and that this need will address itself to a healing ministry. The tentative formulation of ultimate generalities is part of the imaginative freedom granted the communion of possibility. The dialectical function of language carries the community forward as it submits itself to the hermeneutic of the word of God.

IV

It should now be very clear that the proclamation of the word of God is not limited to the sermon. In fact, a living ministry seeks a context in which the word is allowed to become an event. The dialectical power of the word of God naturally directs ministry into the world which it interprets. The actual formulations of ministry have the particularities of real situations. The uniqueness of every situation enriches the meaning of the interpretive power of the word of God. The practical formulation of a pastoral theology is an inheritance of accumulated experiences from the daily life of the church. The interpretive power of the word of God conjoined with the pluralism of experience expands the meaning of ministry beyond any textbook definitions. The ministry must necessarily be viewed as an open-ended vocation.

The practical definition of the ministry is always an experimental definition functionally determined by our involvement in the world. The ministry of the word must not let itself be circumscribed by convention. Paul offers a practical corollary to the prophetic principle when he says "Do not ruin the work of God for the sake of food." (Romans 14:20) We cannot let the practical expression of past ministry obscure the possibilities for a future ministry. The ministry of proclamation must recognize its vocational definition in the word-event. Then it must be flexible enough to transcend institutional expectations and be directed into the world. The topography of sacred markings is a clear indicator that ministry must leave the sanctuary and find its primary home in the world that it addresses.

Thus, the parish ministry makes sense only if the parish is understood as the dwelling place of our experience or as the neighborhood in which life is actualized. The disconnection of the church from where we live out our lives violates the concept of a ministry of proclamation. When the parish is identified with a "congregation" of believers isolated in a sanctuary from the realities of everyday life, the interpretive power of ministry is denied its incarnation. Then a very specialized ministry of reconciliation is required to return us to the business of living. In this case the power of the word of God directs us outside of the congregation back into the parish or neighborhoods where we live.

The style of ministry is individualized by the context in which it is realized. The minister with personal strengths and weaknesses is a constitutive part of this context. A theoretical treatise that transcendentally examines the possibility and meaning of language usage cannot prescribe a formula for successful ministry. What should be clear, however, is that the significance of the word-event extends far beyond the content of proclamation and that conventional formulations of the ministry which elevate the word of God above the realities of daily life actually obstruct the work of God.

The shape of Christian life is not an abstraction determined by theologians. The communion of possibility is a living organism that emerges out of the decisions of ordinary people that live in a world illuminated by the interpretive power of the word-event.

Because we defined religion as the human response to moments of transcendence we must now understand Christian ministry as the qualification of these significant times by the hermeneutic of the word of God. The fabric of ministry is supplied by the experience to which it addresses itself. Reinhold Niebuhr's claim that "without ethical experience the infinite is never defined in ethical terms," is a profound statement about the nature of a vital ministry.[8] The interpretive power of the word of God can never disclose the deeper significance of the comic, ludic, poetic, cosmic, dramatic, oneiric and neurotic dimensions of experiencing without touching these regions of life.

The primary characteristic of a ministry of proclamation that is invarient across the particularities of its realization is its fundamental engagement with the world. A ministry that is isolated in the sanctuary and bound to the pulpit is forgetful of the interpretive power of the word of God that was brought into the world through the Christ-event. Only a ministry that is directly involved with the actualities of daily life can allow the word to become event. When possibility is conjoined with actuality we are then concretely carried into a new future and experience life together as a communion of possibility.

Notes

1. James Dittes, "Who Calls Us Healer?", *The Christian Ministry* (July, 1972), Vol. 3, No. 4.
2. Karl Barth, *The Word of God and the Word of Man* (New York: Harper Torchbooks, 1957), p. 110.
3. Cf. Gerhard Ebeling, *Theology and Proclamation* (Philadelphia: Fortress Press, 1966),. p. 28.
4. Paul Tillich, *Systematic Theology,* 3 vols. (Chicago: University of Chicago Press, 1951, 1957, 1963), Vol. II, pp. 176-180.
5. Several books have recently appeared which assess the theological importance of play and festivity, e.g. Harvey Cox, *The Feast of Fools* (New York: Harper & Row, 1969); Hugo Rahner, *Man at Play* (New York: Herder and Herder, 1967); David L. Miller, *Gods and Games: Towards a Theology of Play* (New York: World Publishing Co., 1970); Sam Keen, *To A Dancing God* (New York: Harper & Row, 1970).
6. See Dietrich Bonhoeffer, *Ethics* (New York: Macmillan Paperback Edition, 1965), "The Last Things and the Things Before the Last," pp. 120-188.
7. *Ibid.,* p. 158.
8. Reinhold Niebuhr, *Leaves From the Notebook of a Tamed Cynic* (Cleveland: The World Publishing Co., Meridan Books, 1957), p. 76.

CHAPTER IX

THE COMMUNION
OF POSSIBILITY

*T*he hermeneutic of the word of God fundamentally contributes to a reinterpretation of the doctrine of the church as well as the concept of ministry. The concept of the church is centered around the word of God in both dogmatic and foundational theology. The mission and justification of the church is the proclamation of the word of God. Thus, a mature assessment of the doctrine of the church must be derived from the dialectical understanding of the content and act of proclamation.

The shift in dogmatic theology from the tendency to view the church as the kingdom of God to an understanding of the church as the people of God emphasizes the importance of the word-event.[1] The church is viewed in a process of becoming that is informed by the content of the word-event and is transformed by the ontological power of the act of proclamation. It is the presence of the word of God in the life of the community that links the church to the historical ministry of Jesus and gives the church eschatological significance as the body of Christ.

In our analysis of the relationship between word and sacrament it was stated that the preaching and life of Jesus gave concreteness and visibility to the love and will of God within the fellowship of disciples. The recognition of Jesus as the Christ was the primary sacrament of the encounter with God. The church was thought to be necessary as a prolongation of sacramental visibility because the fellowship with the historical Jesus is no longer a living possibility. We accordingly recognized that the sacraments are vehicles for the manifestation of God's concern and give continuing visibility to the reality of the resurrected Christ. However, we have delayed our investigation into the nature of the fellowship of disciples that participate in the primary sacrament of the word of God. Beyond the structural recognition of the need for the continuing manifestation of the love of God through its embodiment in the church, we can now look to the hermeneutic of the word of God for an interpretive disclosure of the nature of the church. We could not investigate the doctrine of the church without a theological hermeneutic because the word of God establishes the community. It is the function of the word of God that gives this community its unique character. Not only the invisible church but even the empirical church is the body of Christ because it possesses God's word. As Bonhoeffer has said in *The Communion of Saints*, "The Word is the absolute authority present in the church."[2] The ecclesial mystery is a function of the interpretive power of the word. The presence of the sacrament of the word of God initiates a dialogical mode of existence and thereby establishes a communion that fully participates in the dialectics of a word-event.[3] This communion is assigned its basic character by the functioning and significance of language. Because the ontological significance of language resides in the conjunction of actuality and possibility the church is essentially involved in the disclosure and realization of ontological possibilities. Foundational theology ascertains the multiplicity of language functions and views the ontological function as the primary meaning of a word-event. Thus, it basically views the church as a communion of possibility. That is, the church can have many meanings but it is at least a communion of possibility. The communion of possibility is ontologically descriptive of the nature of the church in foundational theology and it is a regulative conception in the dogmatic description of the church.

Traditional discussions of ecclesiology in dogmatic theology are all to be subordinated to the hermeneutic of the word of God and must not dissolve the ontological importance of the church as a communion of possibility. Before dogmatic theology can proceed with a discussion of the structure of the church, the catholicity of the church, the offices of the church, the sacraments of the church, the mission of the church or any other ecclesiastical concerns, it should be attentive to the foundational analysis of the church as grounded in the authority of the word-event and as a full participant in the dynamics of language functioning. Foundational theology illuminates the existential and ontological meaning of the church.

I

In its foundational meaning the dimensions of the church are determined by the locus of the hermeneutic of the word of God. Thus, the church is not identifiable with institutional limits nor is it denied its manifestation in institutional structures. The church exists wherever there is a ministry of proclamation. The communion of dialogical participation in the word is an establishment and visible expression of the body of Christ.

The church exists because there is a community that confesses that God has revealed his word and that the community possesses this revelation. Dogmatic theology believes in the importance of the church because it believes in the meaningfulness of the content of proclamation; foundational theology confirms the reality of the church because it confirms the meaningfulness of the act of proclamation. The reality of the church is seen whenever the word of God is introduced into the normal processes of language usage. In foundational theology the ontological dynamics of life together in the church can be described in the analysis of language functioning that has the specificity of the content of the language used in the proclamation of the word of God. Of course, foundational theology can never exhaust the conception of the church through an ontological analysis because the ontological significance of the word of God is only one of many meanings determined by the multiple uses of language. But the ontological function is the deepest meaning of language usage and is of primary concern for the adjudication of reality. Thus, "the communion of possibility" is a root metaphor for the existence of the church and it can be embellished and extended by complementary phenomenological investigations of other language functions in the proclamation of the word of God.

The notion of possibility in the metaphor, "the communion of possibility," functions ontologically. That is, possibility refers to forms that ingress into the becoming of actual entities and makes them determinate in the pattern of their realization. The relevant introduction of new forms is the possibility for passage into novel determinations of actuality. They make possible the transcendence of the given in the formation of a new being. The presence of possibility is the transcendental ground for change and the existence of the community that can formatively contribute to the realization of a hopeful future. From the philosophical analysis of hermeneutics we became aware that it is in language functioning that possibility is conjoined with given actualities. To be more precise we said that the propositional structure of language has its ontological analogue which is necessary for the mere continuation of process and is explanatory of the becoming of newly emergent occasions. The continuity of identity and the introduction of novelty are functions of the propositional structure. Secondly, we recognized that the propositional structure on the surface of language is a reflection of the deeper ontological structure and that it functions to augment the complexity of its own foundation in the process of realization. The conscious use of language contributes to the ontological function and intensifies the contrast with possibility by enlarging the scope of actuality present to experience. The concrete uses of language arouse feelings that are part of the subjectivity of becoming in the contrast between subject and predicate in the ontological passage to a new actuality.[4] By contrast on the surface of linguistic experience, the range of actuality can be transformed into an originative ground for the disclosure of possibilities that are ontologically integrated through a predicative pattern. Thus, the concrete expressions of language contribute to the imaginative freedom of deeper ontological movements. The complicity between language usage and its ontological foundation has a double vector quality. The ontological propositional structure allows for the conscious construction of a language and the use of the language augments the complexity of the underlying structure in the movement toward novel actualization.

Foundational studies suggest that in reality it is not only the church that should be viewed as a communion of possibility but that any community established around language usage has this ontological character. Theological inquiry continues by seeking to understand the uniqueness of the church as a communion of possibility. Foundational theology must here be complemented by insights from dogmatic theology into the particularity of the content of Christian proclamation.

The meaning of community which is formed around a language-event is bound by the limits internal to the particular linguistic paradigm that has attracted an assemblage of followers. This was clearly the case in our discussion of scientific communities. The articulation of a paradigm contains a promise of a more meaningful understanding that is sufficiently unprecedented to warrant commitment to the paradigm and initiate a life together. In some cases the life together is no more than a loose association of scholars. The intention or goal of the community which is the reason for its existence is to be discovered in the nature of the promise. The promise is at least an implicit recognition that new possibilities for understanding and actualization are part of the grant of language contained within the paradigm. The range of possibilities open to the articulation of the paradigm is relative to the range of questions sanctioned by the existence of the paradigm. Thus the community exists under a provisional horizon determined by the farthest reaches of acceptable inquiry deemed relevant by the paradigm. The actualization of possibilities within the life of the community cannot exceed its provisional horizon without ceasing to be itself. The adjustment to existential realities in the followship of the community can be no more satisfying than is allowed by a provisional concern under a restricted horizon unless there is recourse to the dynamics of an alternative community.

The discussion of limits and distortions in a topography of sacred markings suggests that secular communities of inquiry always live under provisional horizons and in themselves cannot be ultimately satisfying. The pure desire to know which can find satisfaction only in the complete set of answers to the complete set of questions transcends the limits of secular scientific or philosophical paradigms. This means that the life of a community formed under a secular paradigm is never self contained and it is an aberration of its significance to evaluate its meaning in relationship to the unrestricted desire to know. Secular communities are justified by their realizations of restricted ends.

The presence of the pure desire to know in intellectual patterns of experience is a claim upon society for the need of a community that exists under an ultimate horizon. This is not the only manifestation of need for such a community but it is a tangible and articulate expression of hope for a community to be formed around a word-event that contains a grant of language that is unrestricted in its acceptance of questions formulated out of the full range of actual experience. We have a human need for an empirical community that can accept us where we are and sanction the actualization of possibilities for what we can be. Can we be hearers of a word that offers itself as an originative ground for a communion of possibility and takes us beyond the provisional significance of secular communities? We must assess whether there is a paradigm of hope in the proclamation of the word of God that justifies the formation of a community that can live under an unrestricted horizon. Since an unrestricted paradigm is beyond the achievements of restricted inquiry, we are in fact asking if there has been in our collective experience the manifestation of a word-event that can be the foundation of a community of ultimate concern. Is there any ground for the assertion that there is a communion of possibility that is of ultimate significance?

The history of religions bears witness to the presence of multiple hierophanies that ultimately claim the lives of a people and are the foundation for new communities. These communities understand themselves as ultimately significant.

Many examples could be cited that demonstrate either the explicit formation of a community around a word-event or the importance of a grant of language found in sacred texts that inform the development of a religious community. The accomplishment of the Vedic literature altered the seat of existence in the development of Indian religious traditions and communities. The conjunction of mission and message in the *Rasuliyyah* of Muhammed introduced into Arabic tribalism a new principle that gives priority to the faith relationship over blood relationships and is the foundation for a new universal community. The establishment of a covenant between Jahweh and Abraham was the foundation for a new nation that was further shaped and sometimes chastened by continued revelations of God's word in the prophetic tradition. In Christianity the Christ-event is equated with a word-event. "So the Word became flesh; he came to dwell among us, and we saw his glory, such glory as befits the Father's only Son, full of grace and truth." (John 1:14) In each case the significance of the community is bound up with the significance of the word-event.

In the Christian community the centrality of the word-event to the definition of the church is a pronounced concern. The witness and confession of the Christian community is that in the Christ-event a word of ultimate significance entered the human community. After the Christ-event, the disclosure of possibility could occur under an ultimate horizon. The dynamics of life together are no longer contained by a provisional horizon but can have unlimited significance under the revelation of an unconditional horizon. Thus, the communion of possibility that can bear witness to the resurrected Christ is a community of ultimate concern.

The word of God that founds the Christian community is first present in the proclamation of Jesus that the Kingdom of God is at hand. The word of God is a word of forgiveness or a word of acceptance. The Kingdom of God is at hand in spite of the unfaithfulness of a community. We are granted the courage to view life against an ultimate horizon even though an infinite distance separates our conditioned selves from the unconditional reality of God. Through the word of acceptance the unconditional reality of God is experienced under the image of unconditional love instead of under the image of unconditional judgment. The community has been given the grace to live with an ultimate concern without coming to a perfection or living in fear of harsh judgment.

The word of acceptance sanctions the possibility for radical questioning. That is, the unrestricted desire to know that moves toward an ultimate horizon does not threaten the life of a community that is rooted in God's word of acceptance. The word-event gives us the courage to see ourselves as conditioned below an unconditional horizon. The vision of transcendence sought for in the unrestricted desire to know is no longer a forbidden mystery. The community of the word of God allows us to take seriously the full range of possibilities announced through the acceptance of actuality. The judgment of possibility upon the incompleteness of actuality draws us into a new creativity against the background of an unlimited horizon. We are supported in the risk of a conjunction of possibility with actuality by the collective courage of our life together in a community of acceptance. The courage of the community is the ethical foundation for a new consciousness and that courage is born out of the proclamation of the word of God.

The community of ultimate concern that is founded by the incarnate disclosure of the word of God is bound up with the dynamics of language functioning. Thus, the revelation of the word of God founds a community and gives rise to thought. The consciousness of the community rooted in the conjunction of actuality and possibility is the embryonic beginning of a theological tradition. The centrality of the word-event and the characterization of the community as a communion of possibility ascertains the place of theology in the growth of Christian fellowship.

The word of acceptance is not a new subject matter for theological investigation. It is the disclosure of an unlimited horizon under which the unrestricted desire to know is given a proper sanction. The dialectical participation in transcendence through the elementary raising of further questions is a concrete achievement of meaning that progressively alters the visible expression of Christian discipleship. Life together in a communion of possibility receives its self consciousness from the ontological dynamics of language functioning. The vision of the nearness or presence of God in the topography of sacred markings is made possible by the proclamation of the word of God. But this vision is not given as a sacred object to be looked at in the moment of acceptance. It is a work to be achieved through the dialectical functioning of language. The word that is given gives rise to theology. Theology is part of the cost of discipleship. That is, the hermeneutic of the word of God interprets experience so that we can find the reality of God in the world. This theological achievement is part of what it means to be a disciple of Christ. It is part of the glory of life in Christ.

It should be clear that theology is not an accessory of Christian fellowship that can be used to embellish the worship experience. The ontological connection between thinking and being places theology in the center of Christian life. Theology must be represented in the communion of possibility to place language in the service of our fellowship. Theology asks the questions that carry thought and experience toward an ultimate horizon. Since it is the unique function of language to give rise to expanded experience, it is the unique function of theology to articulate and thematize an ultimate concern so that language carries us toward an experience of ultimate significance. The grant of language that gives rise to theological reflection is transformed by the carrying function of language into an experience whereby we can even recognize the resurrected Christ in the stranger we meet on our road to Emmaus.

The reality consciousness of the church as a communion of possibility is unlimited in principle because the conjunction of actuality with the full range of possibility is not artifically limited by a provisional horizon. The church should be exemplary in the struggle for reality because it alone is a communion of possibility that can sanction the logical questions of theological inquiry. The church can risk the freedom of inquiry that carries us to the boundaries of experience because the word of God has transformed the disclosure of ultimate reality from judgment to acceptance of our finite being in the world.

Within the life of the church, theology has its functional specialties but all of these specialities function dialectically.[5] That is, theology contributes to the formation of a new being by itsself transcendent participation in the act of knowing. Theology positions our being in the world and foundationally contributes to the becoming of a new actuality. Thus, theology is not a secondary reflection on the life of the community. It is a primary constituent in the passage toward the future. This is an ontological consideration from the general theory of language functioning. In the theological use of language the passage into a future actuality is directed toward an ultimate horizon.

The significance of theology is not limited to any particular theological tradition but is a characteristic of theological inquiry in general. The dialectic between the content and act is a corrective movement that issues forth in a call for expanded experience. Theology is the visible manifestation of activity within the communion of possibility that lives under an unlimited horizon. Theology is the issue of the word-event in which language is allowed to function dialectically.

Theology is the embodiment of the hermeneutic of the word of God in the communion of possibility. Theology facilitates a dialogical mode of existence and gives a concrete expression to the interpretive power of proclamation. It is concerned with the very existence of fellowship in the communion of possibility and can be viewed as an existential modality for the continuing manifestation of the sacred.[6] In the communion of possibility, theology is a movement of thought stamped with the excitement of self realization.

II

The conception of the church as a communion of possibility portrays the fellowship of disciples as radically free and open to the future. The church is here viewed as a paradigm of freedom within the more restrictive institutions of society. The word of acceptance grounds the courage to risk an openness to an ultimate horizon in the realization of individuation processes. The proclamation of the word of God is no less than an invitation to the fullness of an authentic selfhood.

The hermeneutic of the word of God reveals the possibilities for a community that enriches experience and carries its members beyond the immediacies of history toward an eschatological meaning. We may, however, ask whether this conception of fellowship can be realistically conjoined with the actuality of experience in the empirical church. Can the hermeneutic of the word of God transform the empirical church into a communion of possibility? The claim that we have made for the existence of the church is that only in a community of ultimate concern can we nourish the ontological processes that bring about a full realization of the authentic self. The contrasting opinion in secular thought is that the church and even religion in general forestalls experience and sometimes falsifies the reality of the human condition. Within the religious community we often hear the parallel opinion that the institutional church gets in the way of the ministry of the word of God. For these reasons it is very tempting in the face of secular criticism to identify the communion of possibility with the invisible church. But this is a failure to understand the dialectical involvement of the word-event with the world. Possibility must be conjoined with actuality in the passage toward a new being. The communion of possibility has no ontological significance unless it is an empirical community accepting of the givenness of actuality. To deny the church its incarnation is to deny the word of God its interpretive power that offers a healing grace to the world.[7]

The conception of the church as a communion of possibility does not identify the church with the kingdom of God. The church is the people of God and it is in the process of becoming. The dimensions of the church are determined by the locus of the hermeneutic of the word of God. The church will be weak and sinful in its becoming because the ministry of proclamation is directed into the world. The hope of the church is the promise of the word that its finiteness before an infinite horizon is received with acceptance instead of judgment. It is the promise of the word of God that allows us to celebrate the reality of the church.

Abandoning the doctrine of the church that too easily identifies the church with the kingdom of God is the first step in freeing the church to fully enter the dynamics of worldly life. The church can live on a multiplicity of levels when it is not bound to the illusion of perfection. In the communion of possibility the reality of hope is not hearsay but is conjoined with the actual occasions that mark our presence in the world.

We are still combating the docetic heresy that denies the word of God its human embodiment. The need for Christological formulations that insisted that Jesus Christ was fully God and fully man extends to the doctrine of the church as the continuing manifestation of God's love. The church must also be a conjunction of the human and the divine. In our formulation of this union we have said that the hermeneutic of the word of God interprets the world to which it is addressed and thereby determines the locus of the church. The fabric of the church's experience is a conjunction of actuality with possibility under an ultimate horizon.

Claims of perfection or identity with the kingdom of God are signs of resistence to the humanity of the church. The kingdom of God is at hand, but it must not be used to disguise the realities of human experience that can be transformed by the power of the word-event. The word of God should be allowed to dialectically participate in the topography of sacred markings and not be used to mask the natural quest for self transcendence.

A church which defines itself as a communion of possibility cannot be true to itself if it ignores the reality of suffering and the dark side of human existence. We cannot have a theology of glory without the theology of the cross. The church can risk the cross because it lives under an ultimate horizon that gives meaning beyond the grave. The actual fellowship of disciples should be marked by the willingness to confront the night as well as celebrate the vision of a new day.

The church as a communion of possibility is the institution in which the human condition is to be shared in depth.[8] The conjunction of possibility with actuality in the dialectical functioning of language intensifies and alters the consciousness of actuality. The grant of language resident in the life of the church has the power to heighten joy and confront evil in a context of meaning that transcends the moment. We come to possess our feelings within conscious experience rather than have them operate upon us as unknown forces.

The prophetic function of the church that discloses new possibilities that judge the present also invites us into a new future with a word of acceptance. The prophetic function of the word of God is conjoined with the priestly function through the dialectical power of language. The transformation of experience in a new consciousness is a healing ministry. We can share on increasingly deeper levels the critical moments of our development. The liturgy that accompanies life together is directly concerned with understanding and transforming the community's experience of birth, puberty, marriage, vocations, aging, sickness, and death.[9] The crises of life unfold in the communion of possibility under an ultimate horizon. The significance of life is magnified when it is felt as part of the larger movement entailed in self transcendence.

The interpretation of experience within the church directly addresses itself to a question of ultimate meaning. Are we related to something infinite or not? The word of acceptance establishes the context in which such a question can be asked.

Carl Jung thinks that this is the decisive question of life.[10] Only when we can interpret life under an ultimate horizon can we avoid investing our lives in trivialities. The hermeneutic of the word of God revalorizes the critical moments of life in the fullness of their meanings. The communion of possibility is the originative ground for a new consciousness and the becoming of a more satisfying reality. Jung struggled with the church because it was not a communion of possibility. The decisive question of life was not accepted in the church theology of his experience because radical questioning threatened the mask of perfection that haunted the community of believers. It is only when we become hearers of the word of acceptance that the church can understand itself as the communion of possibility that sanctions the dialectical function of language usage. In this dialectical function the word of God has prophetic and priestly efficacy. The church can accept the thrust of an unrestricted desire to know. The reality that transcends that achievement of the present is the reality that judges the adequacy of the moment but also accepts the present into a movement toward a more satisfying future.

It is the present or concreteness of the moment that is conjoined with possibility in the language functioning of the hermeneutic of the word of God. Thus, the topography of sacred markings is a practical guide for organizing to meet the institutional needs of a church as it expands its boundaries and approaches the dimensions of a communion of possibility. The practical ministry that proclaims the word of God must reflect on the contours of experience in the administration of pastoral responsibilities. Decisions must be made that provide the occasion for hearing of the word. Permission must be given visible expression for pursuing the unrestricted desire to know. There are practical considerations that contribute to the readiness to become hearers of the word of acceptance. The revelation of God must be received and the conditions of reception provide the fabric and form of the revelatory event.

Practical ministry cannot ignore the fabric and form of the word-event. We must even consider what times in the life of a people, in their individual and collective development, move to the edges of conceptual achievement and seek for a language that can adequately express the meaning of the moment. These times are ready for the hermeneutic of the word of God. These times are drawn into the communion of possibility and constitute the deepest meanings of liturgical celebration among the fellowship of disciples. The responsibility of ministry is to prepare the community to receive moments of crisis and happiness into its celebration and worship. The topography of sacred markings is an elementary guide to the richness of moments in the passage of time.

The church has tried not to neglect its priestly function. The dramatic rendering of experience has a traditional place in the life of the church. The church has addressed itself to birth, puberty, marriage, vocations, aging, sickness and death in the formulation of sacraments and liturgical practice. The genius of religion is evidenced in the history of symbols that have long accompanied the dramatic passage through life. The communion of possibility extends the vision of the church and also recognizes the need to participate in the ludic, comic, poetic, oneiric, cosmic and neurotic regions of experiencing. The church must be playful and accept the meaning of play into its fellowship. But it must also introduce the healing power of the word of God into the confines of neurotic experience. This means that a practical ministry must organize structures and provide a place where even the neurotic personality can become a hearer of the word of God. This place is not necessarily the sanctuary and the word of God is not necessarily tied to the sermon. The hermeneutic of the word of God defines the role of ministry and originates the communion of possibility but the shape of ministry and the institutionalization of the church for the meaningful extension of ministry is the imaginative achievement of the fellowship of disciples. Whether the church meets in a house, storefront, or traditional sanctuary should be determined by the needs of the community. Whether the church worships around a sermon or within the conversations of small groups is also relative to the needs of the community and is not determined by the hermeneutic of the word of God. The institutionalization of the church and the ministry secures the occasion for the word-event. The consciousness of the importance of the word-event is reinforced by vocational responsibility and is protected by the planning of the community. The success of organization in the institutional church is accompanied by failure, but that failure is subsumed into the dialectical processes of language functioning in the creation of a new reality. The communion of possibility must not be denied its incarnation in the empirical church, but yet it always transcends its embodiment. The reality of the communion of possibility is historical and eschatological.

III

The historical reality of the church has been reclaimed in the shift from viewing the church as the kingdom of God to viewing it as the people of God. The people of God are allowed their humanity and are not distorted by images of perfection. The church is in the process of development and the people are on a pilgrimage. Jürgen Moltmann refers to the communion of possibility as the "Exodus Church" to focus attention on the fellowship of Christians as the movement of a pilgrim people.[11] The freedom of this people is granted by the promise of the future. It is an eschatological hope that carries the significance of the community beyond its historical achievement.

I agree that the church is distinguished from other institutions because it is an eschatological community, but I do not think that we can adequately analyze the eschatological reality of the communion of possibility by only examining the content of promise in the history of revelation. The conception of the church in foundational theology is grounded in the ontological significance of the dialectical function of language usage and the uniqueness of religious language. Foundational theology suggests that the communion of possibility is an eschatological community when the horizon of possibility is unconditional. Ecclesiology is subject to the foundational insight that eschatology has ontological as well as historical meaning. Thus, foundational theology complements Moltmann's conception of the "Exodus Church" with an ontological analysis of the communion of possibility. In ontological analysis, an eschatological reality has been equated with reality at the ultimate horizon and that horizon has been located through the conception of an unrestricted desire to know as the horizon of being itself. The communion of possibility can be viewed as an eschatological community when it promotes a movement to the horizon of being.

Since the conception of being that we have been using to illuminate the notion of an ultimate horizon has been drawn from the natural experience of an unrestricted desire to know, it is itself unrestricted or unconditional. That is, there are no conditioning determinates that can be used in defining the nature of being. It is simply beyond any limiting notions of intelligibility. Of particular importance for our immediate discussion is the recognition that the horizon of being lays beyond the determinations of any spatial-temporal coordinate systems. Thus, a movement to the horizon of being is a movement beyond the limitations of time and space.

The doctrine of final things can be understood as a doctrine of ultimate things. Finality is an image of ultimacy as well as a temporal determination. In fact, when we refer to the horizon of being, no temporal determination can be made, and, therefore, finality can only mean ultimacy. Eschatological realities can be translated to mean ultimate realities. The communion of possibility is an eschatological community when the word of God discloses the dimension of ultimacy in the interpretation of existence.

Even when we use the popular religious conception of the "end of time," we discover a multiplicity of meanings that point toward an ontological understanding of eschatology. The end of time may refer to the last moment or it may refer to the end of temporality as a limiting form for the manifestation of reality. When time is spatialized, the end of time is usually thought to refer to the last marked increment to include the final point on an artificial line. Eschatology is here transformed into a spatial conception and fails to relate to the lived experience of time. Spatial conceptions of time and eschatology are abstractions imposed upon lived experience instead of realities interpretively disclosed within experience. The eloquent arguments of Henri Bergson which claim that introducing a linear conception of space into the conception of duration corrupts our experiences of change, movement, and freedom are extended in our discussion to the claim that the spatialization of time corrupts an understanding of eschatology.[12] The end of time which is viewed as the end of a line must be reconceived to comprehend the end of temporality as a limiting condition imposed upon objective experience and understanding. In ontological eschatology, time is transcended and not extended. Foundational theology views the church as an eschatological community because the word-event overcomes the power of time. The consciousness of an eschatological community is the consciousness of meanings that transcend the contingencies of history. This consciousness is a dialectical achievement of the word of God.

The church is an eschatological community because it is determined by the locus of the hermeneutic of the word of God. This word interprets existence so that we can view reality under the fullness of an unconditional horizon. Because the word of God is a word of acceptance, the church can accept the movement of an unrestricted quest for understanding that carries us toward the reality of being itself. The word of God grants us the courage and power to see a richer vision of reality.

This is actually an ontological consideration. The expansion of our consciousness of reality is a metaphysical achievement and not merely an epistemological clarification. The church is conceptualized as a communion of possibility rooted in the proclamation of the word of God, because it is through the dialectical power of language that the realities of actuality and possibility are conjoined in the passage toward a new being and in the achievement of a new consciousness. The word of acceptance allows the conjunction of actuality with an unlimited horizon of possibility. The judgment of unlimited possibility upon the meager realization of past actuality is transformed into new complexity rather than being the mere dissolution of an old identity. The limited achievements of meaning under the conditions of history are viewed by an eschatological consciousness as manifestations of an ultimate meaning. This ultimate meaning is not bound by history, but is manifested within history. Ultimate meaning is a condition of the unlimited possibility that can be approached through the release of an unrestricted desire to know by the word of acceptance.

The church as a communion of possibility secures a larger vision of reality for our culture. More importantly, the church implements the movement toward the actualization of a larger reality by housing the hermeneutic of the word of God. The new consciousness nourished within the life of the church is a manifestation of a new actuality nourished within the life of the church.

In the fellowship of the church the word of God is given a concrete locus. The communion of possibility embodies the hermeneutic power of the word of God. Thus, the empirical church is an expression of an immediate actuality that can be transformed in the dialectic of language functioning into a new being. The church addresses our actuality by allowing a vision of possibility. The church is at once a historical movement and an eschatological reality.

The kingdom of God is at hand in the fellowship of the church. The victory of Christ affirmed the significance of actuality under the horizon of unconditional possibility. The resurrection of the Christ transformed the fellowship of Jesus with his disciples into a prolepsis of the future. That future is realized throughout the passage of history in the continuing life of the church. Thus, foundational and dogmatic theology conspire to claim that whenever the hermeneutic of the word of God is given a home, the fellowship of disciples is a communion of possibility.

NOTES

1. See E. Schillebeeckx, *God the Future of Man* (New York: Sheed and Ward, 1968), pp. 121, 128; and Karl Rahner *et al.,* eds., *Sacramentum Mundi,* Vol. I (New York: Herder and Herder, 1968), p. 348.
2. Dietrich Bonhoeffer, *The Communion of Saints* (New York: Harper and Row, 1963), p. 173.
3. E. Schillebeeckx, *God the Future of Man,* p. 128; "The Church's ministry is the sacrament of mankind's dialogical mode of existence." This claim of Schillebeeckx becomes ontologically significant because of our conception of language functioning.
4. For my technical discussion of the relationship between the ontic and ontological functions of language, see Charles E. Winquist, *The Transcendental Imagination* (The Hague: Martinus Nijhoff, 1972), pp. 71-75.

5. See Bernard Lonergan, *Method of Theology* (New York: Herder and Herder, 1972), for a mature assessment of functional specialties in theology using a transcendental method for analysis.
6. Charles E. Winquist, "Theology and the Manifestation of the Sacred," *Theological Studies*, Vol. 32, No. 1, March 1971.
7. For clarification of this point see E. Schillebeeckx, *Christ the Sacrament of the Encounter with God* (New York: Sheed and Ward, 1963), p. 203. "Again and again men have fallen into the heresy of regarding the Church as merely the invisible communion of those who truly live in the union of grace with Christ. They deny the Church its incarnation. They take away not only its weakness and sinfulness but also the visibility of its grace, which means that they take away grace itself."
8. cf. Richard Rubenstein, *After Auschwitz* (Indianapolis: Bobbs-Merrill, 1966), p. 154.
9. *Ibid.*, p. 146. Rubenstein thinks that the appropriate function of the rabbi is priestly. "Their role is to help the individual pass through the crises of life with appropriate rituals which have the power to alleviate the conflicts inherent in the worst moments and heighten the joys of the best."
10. Carl Jung, *Memories, Dreams, Reflections* (New York: Random House, Vintage Books, 1963), p. 325.
11. Jürgen Moltmann, *Theology of Hope* (New York: Harper and Row, 1967), p. 304.
12. Henri Bergson, *Time and Free Will* (New York: Harper Torchbooks, 1960), p. 74.

INDEX

Dittes, James, 118
Docetic heresy, 143
Dogmatic theology, 17, 29-31, 33-36, 38,
  45, 46, 93, 103, 108, 109,
  133-136, 149
Dramatic, 16, 71, 74, 75, 80, 83, 96, 125,
  127, 131, 145
Duration, 148

Easter, 113, 114
Ebeling, Gerhard, 101, 104
Ecclesial mystery, 134
Ecclesiology, 134, 147
Ecstasy, 122
Ecstatic communion, 122, 123
Ego, 82
Eidetic reduction, 55
Einstein, Albert, 87
Eliade, Mircea, 20, 28, 67
Emmaus Road, 21-24, 27, 105, 140
Empirical church, 134, 142, 146, 149
Enlightenment, 120
Epiphany, 110, 112
Epochal occasions, 51, 54
Epoche, 100
Eschatological: community, 22, 118,
  146-148; event, 101; gospel, 101;
  mission, 18; preaching, 109, 110;
  situation, 118
Eschatology, 109, 112, 113, 147, 148
Eternal now, 22
Eternal objects, 52, 53, 82
Eternity, 72, 111
Ether drift, 90
Eucharist, 22
Evil, 143
"Exodus Church," 146, 147

Fallacy of misplaced concreteness, 38
Finality, 147
Folklore, 79
Forgiveness, 139
Foundational: analysis, 16, 134; inquiry,
  15; studies, 136; theology, 14-17,
  29-31, 33-46, 65-67, 81, 84, 87, 88,
  100, 102, 103, 106, 108, 112, 121,
  133-137, 147-149; thinking, 41
Freud, Sigmund, 72, 76, 78, 94
Fuchs, Ernest, 104
Functional specialities, 141
Funk, Robert, 104

Gestalt, 68
Gilkey, Langdon, 46, 93, 113
Glory, 138, 140, 143
Gnostic, 83
Gödel, Kurt, 91
Gospel, 23, 24, 35, 93, 108, 110, 111
Grace, 100, 121, 127, 138, 139, 142
Grave, 143

Healing, 118, 129, 142, 144, 145
Heidegger, Martin, 23, 30, 61, 73
Heuristic, 25, 41, 49-51, 54, 56-57, 63,
  81, 91
Hierophanous, 20, 81, 102, 112, 115
Hierophany, 29, 81, 102, 112, 138
Historian of religions, 74
History of religions, 61, 66, 79, 80, 138
Holocaust, 114
Homo absconditus, 111, 113
Homo ludens, 72, 126
Homo religiosus, 82, 83, 96
Hope, 65, 66, 74, 109, 110, 113-116,
  122, 137, 138, 143, 146
Horizon, 9, 10, 15, 40-44, 46, 63, 92, 95,
  96, 98-100, 111, 137-143, 147-149
Huizinga, Johan, 72
Humor, 126
Hybrid, 58
Hypnosis, 76

Illusion, 62
Imagination, 44, 53
Imaginative patterns of meaning, 50
Immutability, 88
Incarnation, 20, 29, 113, 130, 142
Individuation, 82, 83, 105, 128, 129, 142
Inertial coordinate system, 90
Ingression, 99
Intelligibility, 9, 12, 36-38, 41, 44, 56,
  65, 66, 81, 86, 88, 90-92, 98, 100, 147
Intuition, 38, 45
Invisible church, 134, 142
Isomorphism, 59
Israel, 109, 112, 114

Jahweh, 138
James, William, 55
Jaspers, Karl, 98
Jeremias, Joachim, 101
Jesus, 12, 16, 19-22, 27, 101, 102, 109,
  110, 133, 139
Judeo-Christian, 110

154   *Index*

Notes